Contents

by Mary Rose Donnelly
with research by Heather Dau
in consultation with Kevin Anderson, Lynn Brennan and others

© The Canadian Churches Forum for Global Ministries
Toronto, Ontario 1995

Revised 2007. 2010

The Canadian Churches' Forum is deeply grateful for the generous bequest of Julia Ruby
and dedicates this publication to her memory.

ISBN #0-969-9954-0-7

The illustrations in this booklet are used with permission of Scarborough Missions and the
Office on Global Education for Church World Service. Artist: Sr. Eunice Cudzewicz.

Yahweh
has
sent me
to bring
good news
to the
Poor,
to bind up
hearts
that are
Broken,
to proclaim
Liberty
to
Captives

Isaiah : 61

1. The Start of Something Big

After attending numerous weddings of his friends in the movie *Four Weddings and a Funeral*, a young man, Charles, begins to wonder why he is never the groom. He decides to take the plunge, but while he is standing in the church waiting for his wedding to begin, he meets the woman he knows to be his true love, who is not, lamentably, the one in the veil readying to come up the aisle. In the briefest of conversations he discovers that this woman's recent marriage has failed irreconcilably. And so he is caught in the dilemma of a lifetime. From what we know of Charles, a very polite, reserved British gentleman, he has displayed no particular gift for changing the course of events even when they are four-square in his own interest, so you expect this wedding to sweep him up and destine him to a life of loss and longing.

Ironically, it is his younger brother who stops the wedding. It is a passionate and honest plea from, of all those present, the least likely person. The brother is deaf, and while he cannot communicate as everyone else can, he knows that the train his brother is on must be stopped, while Charles takes some time to think about the decision before him. At the appropriate point, the deaf man halts the service and makes his older brother translate his sign-language message, which, ironically, finally gives Charles the words to articulate what he's truly feeling.

Are you really sure?

Right about now your Aunt Madeleine is writing to get a special dispensation for your canonization; your mother is on Valium; your father is wandering around the house scratching intently at his bald spot; your eldest brother thinks you'll come back with some tropical disease that will leave you dependent on them the rest of your life; and the church women are dedicating their new sink to you. Your old friends step back a yard when you say you will be working with the poor in Tupelo, (Tupelo is everywhere by the way), and quickly change the subject to an exhaustive description of the house renovations they have underway. Meanwhile you're torn between enjoying the fuss of going-away parties and the sheer terror of not knowing where you will be, where you will live, or how you will communicate a month from now. If you've ever changed towns and schools as a child, multiply it by twenty.

Should this make you change your mind? Not necessarily. But there are a few questions you should be asking yourself now to ensure as much as possible that you are making the right choice for yourself and your life at this time. If the wedding is stopped now there will be consequences—disappointments, expressions of low-grade fury and an awful waste of inedible cake—but these will pass and they will be a lot less damaging than entering a commitment that will affect you the rest of your life, as this one will.

Like the person about to be married, you are also on the threshold of one of the most important moments of your life. You, and all those who have coached you to this point in your life and really love you, want it to be the right choice. The train is stopped and you should take whatever you need, a day or a week, find some quiet among the chaos, to carefully examine what it is you are about to take on. Whether you are traveling for a month, volunteering your skills for half a year, or taking on a job in another country for three years or more, this experience will change you. It will provide you with a new set of eyes; ones that will forever see the world differently

When other countries are transformed from those nebulous shapes in an atlas into names and faces of children, men and women whom you've met, struggled with and come to love, you will begin to question the systems and forces that doom many of them to a life of poverty. Things you've read about in theory will become real and present: Infant mortality rates of four in ten children translate into Mrs. Oong's third child. Ultimately you will begin to question a lot that you took for granted in your own culture as well, including those factors that protect Western privilege at the expense of the majority of the people in the world. When you eventually return home, you will see life through new eyes there as well.

The following activities and questions are for your own benefit, to encourage you to do some last pre-plunge reflection on whether or not you are going for the right reasons. Many of the ideas you will see treated in this introduction will be dealt with in depth later on in the booklet, but this will give you a bit of a foretaste of what is before you. We would suggest that you talk about the ideas in this booklet with your partner or a friend, or keep a journal of your reflections. Loan the book to the person you're closest to, so that she or he will get a sense of the issues you are confronting. Another option is to begin writing your feelings and ideas about these questions in letters to someone who will treasure your thoughts and keep them for you as part of a record of this time in your life.

It's all before you

One of the first things you will need to cope with when you are away is difference. For one thing, you will likely be expected to learn a new language. Learning a new way to communicate is in itself a huge challenge, but it is only the tip of the iceberg. Even if you were lucky enough to already share the same language as the people of your new country, cultures can be fraught with subterranean signals and body language that can leave you floundering between the word spoken and the meaning intended.

Try to remember the last time you got into a serious misunderstanding with someone. It can happen when people are close, share some history, similar backgrounds and values. You both heard the same words and you each understood them differently. Fortunately it doesn't happen too often and you both have enough trust in the integrity of the other to know he or she would not deliberately hurt you, yet a misunderstanding has occurred. It happens every day of our lives, language shifts and slides because the words we use, even the every-day variety, often mean different things to different people. What do the words justice, love, caring, commitment, poverty and wealth mean to you? What do you think they mean to Uncle Phil? Or your Sunday school teacher of 25 years ago? What do they mean to the woman who works out with you in aerobics? And the guy who cleans the milking machines on your father's farm? The differences are multiplied when we attempt to string those words into comprehensible speech; it can take years before we understand even simple humour across a culture.

For another thing, chances are you are not going to blend easily in the new culture. As with many people going overseas, the way you look may very well set you apart long before you open your mouth. As soon as you are seen, people may make assumptions about you based on the way you look – facial features, skin colour, height, clothing. They might assume, for example, that you are privileged. Some of their assumptions may be correct, but others will be as unfair as racism is in any shape or form. Many people have only North American movies to inform them of what Westerners are like. It's not pretty. Your outward appearance may help you blend into the culture to which you are being welcomed, but that may mean that the expectations will be higher on you to adjust quickly. If you are third-generation of African, Japanese, or Indian descent, for example, you may be able to speak the language of the people you are to work with, but you may not have the deep cultural understanding and skills to make communication clear or easy.

Some people in our society are indifferent to the way they look—they wear blue jeans with strategic holes to weddings, dye their hair chartreuse, avoid deodorant and pierce their eyebrows. But a multi-billion dollar fashion industry would prove that these folk are the vast minority. We are programmed to blend. Experiment with this one to test your own comfort level with difference. If you usually wear casual clothes to work, wear formal attire, dress to the nines. Or mix and match plaids, bows, sneakers and suspenders the next time you go out for a meal with friends. You will attract stares, to be sure, but this is only the beginning of it. When you walk into a new culture you won't be able to shake the discomfort of standing-out by a quick change of clothes. How important is it for you to fit in?

Fitting in at different levels

There is fitting in and then there is fitting in. You may be aloof to fashion and appearance, but it is very important for you to have your ideas taken seriously. In your own culture, people take you seriously because of the integrity of your work. But working out of a Christian commitment in another country is not always going to be a ticket into the kind of world you might enjoy at home. If you've worked among progressive ecumenical organizations, for example, and enjoyed rubbing elbows with secular and religious feminists, you might be surprised to be kept at arm's length, downright distrusted even, by secular feminists in other countries. If doors have been opened for you because of your religious associations in the past, you may be surprised to encounter suspicion, perhaps even ridicule in a new culture and country.

Christianity has a past. Attempts to grapple with the history of the missionary movement have spawned a number of very worthwhile books in the past decade or two, and one of your siblings will be sure to send them to you for Christmas if you only raise that little finger. A brief overview can be found in Appendices A and B at the back of the book. The story is an astounding lesson that people who meant so well could produce outcomes they never imagined. There is no doubt that tremendous good came out of the selfless work of thousands of the world's brightest, best educated and idealistic men and women; but it is also true that history shows that their efforts were sometimes misguided.

Take the indigenous people of this continent as an example. Throughout much of the 20th Century, the major Canadian denominations ran residential schools for indigenous children. Mostly they were funded by the federal government, with the explicit intention of implementing government policy to assimilate indigenous people into Canadian (that is European-Canadian) society. The children were brought to these boarding schools, sometimes against their will; they were given Christian names and forbidden to speak their languages or to use their indigenous names. The churches and their personnel had every good intention of helping Indigenous people develop the skills necessary to survive economically in a predominantly white society. They taught them about Christianity, they taught them trades, and helped them learn to read and write. They discouraged, sometimes forcefully, any practice of indigenous spirituality, and the children were rarely, if ever, encouraged either overtly or covertly to value their indigenous heritage.

The unintended result was that after eight years of school, children could hardly communicate with their parents, and, perhaps more detrimental than that, they emerged ambivalent about their own culture, ashamed of their indigenous ways. Decades later, indigenous people identify the residential schools as one of the major sources of dysfunction within their lives and communities. Some of the churches have taken steps to begin the healing process that they acknowledge is long-overdue.

Colonialism and Christianity

Historically, overseas mission work has not always had its intended results either. Throughout the 20th century and to the present, many countries struggle to throw off the oppression of colonialism. Independence sometimes required them to take a giant step away from the West and the values it promoted, and sometimes Christianity was included in this. China is one dramatic recent example. In the 1940s, when foreigners with insight in China saw what was down the road, they began to see that it was not right to hold the purse strings and leadership positions in the churches, hospitals, institutions and universities that they had established, and so began grooming Chinese to take up leadership roles in them. But it was too little too late. By the time the Communist revolution swept the country in the 1950's, and it became embarrassing to have anything to do with foreigners, an entire class of Chinese Christians had already evolved that had bettered its economic situation by association with Westerners.

There were cases, of course, where missions led the way of revolt against the colonials. In South America, Spanish Jesuits created the Reductions, highly-sophisticated communal organizations for the Guarani indigenous people. Eventually their success came into conflict with the desire of the colonials for more land and wealth, and the Reductions were ultimately destroyed, as were most of the Guarani and the Jesuits who established them. In many countries of Africa, independence leaders were very often the children of the first generation of indigenous church leaders.

For every country that took a step away from the West in its quest for independence, there were countless others that immediately, or eventually, embraced Western values such as materialism and consumerism—Mickey Mouse, Nike shorts and North American pop music greet you from every market.

You as a newcomer to the culture could experience a smooth or bumpy reception based on this kind of history that has nothing to do with you personally. It will be important for you to get to know the history of your host country before you go there, and begin to understand why, in some situations, the visit or work of any foreigner, however welcome you are to the tourist industry, or the little church or organization you will work with, might be regarded by others with some suspicion and even scorn. If it is important for you to be liked, needed or trusted quickly, you might want to ask yourself if this is the right direction to be taking now or the kind of work to be entering.

Now, of course there is the other side of the coin. Sometimes the inner circle of your work will provide a personality cult for you. No matter what you say or do, people will expect you to be holy and only holy. The men think they have to take off their hats around you and hide the beer. You can do no wrong and the niceness will drive you to distraction. There will be no opportunity to let your hair down and associate with those outside the fold or over the fence. In each of the extremes, and the many shades in between them, it will likely take a while before you find someone to open your heart to.

Not all of that has to do with the difficulty of finding the right person to befriend. The language barrier plays havoc with you. It just so happens that there are levels to learning a new language and the last level you achieve, a long, long time after you are able to grunt the desire to buy bread or eggs, is the ability to express, in words, your feelings. Most of us have more or less trouble expressing our deepest feelings in our first language; add on a new language and the complications of finding the right person to talk to and the struggle to communicate can seem temporarily insurmountable. Plan to talk to yourself a lot in the first few months. However difficult it may be, finding new friends and nurturing older long-distance relationships becomes essential. How we do this depends in large part on how we go—alone, with a partner, friend or family.

Finding support

Dreams are not often shared equally by every member of a family. One partner may feel a profound call to this venture which may not be shared by the other. Or perhaps both parents are eager to go, but teenagers elect to stay behind with grandparents or friends rather than face the upheaval of a new culture and language. If you know that your partner or your children have reservations about this venture, you must find a way of talking about it, which is different from talking them into it. The journey ahead can be sweet with experiences that will move you deeply, but it will also be speckled with some hard and painful times which will only be exaggerated if they are borne with any feelings of resentment for having come *for* someone else. In these days of text-messaging and podcasting, communication is quicker and easier than it has ever been. There may be a way for you to endure a long-distance relationship for a few months while you pursue your dreams, but not at the expense of someone else's.

Between the time that you arrive in Tupelo and the time it takes to find friends, you will need to spend a great deal of time in your own company. Everyone in a family will have their individual struggles in the new situation. Take away all those familiar extended supports from home and you'll find there might not be as much time, will or ability to care for one another as you would wish. It's okay if you're up and your partner is down and you can be the supportive, tender friend you consider yourself to be. What happens when you and your partner are both just barely treading the emotional waters? It's then that we're flung back on our solitude. Can you be alone? Do you like to be alone? Do you only want to be alone? Obviously, extremes are not desirable but chances are good that you will confront your aloneness more than you've ever done in the past.

These questions are equally applicable to single people. While their situation may be enviable to married people who have the responsibility of helping a partner and children adjust to the new culture, singleness does come with a price. Many cultures are so family-oriented that you will feel out of place without children or a spouse to tend and to talk about. Nor will you have the comfort of a companion from the outset who knows you well and with whom you can share your concerns and insecurities.

Life in another country will probably be easier for you if you tend to be comfortable with your solitude. Whether you go as a couple, a single person, or a family, you can still feel very alone in a foreign world— oh for a good cup of tea, an afternoon with your sister-in-law, a piece of raspberry pie. It's hard to be without the old-faithful comforts and confidantes

Decision in the eye of the storm

At times like that, when you are without your regular supports, you may begin to experience exaggerations in your normal emotional dips and jumps. How well do you understand your own moods, and what kinds of safeguards do you place on decisions made during those times, for example, that sudden desire you have to make a career of salmon fishing off the Fraser River? You've never fished before in your life.

There is a temptation, when we're unhappy with our lives, to shake out the most incoherent option and see it writ in glittering lights. Usually, the second sober thought of a new day makes us thankful for flight cancellation insurance. If you already experience highs and lows that set you reeling for a few days, the chances are very good that they will be more pronounced and debilitating when you are away from familiar territory and people.

Worse than the blues by far, however, is the prospect that *this* decision to travel or work in another country is a temptation equivalent to salmon fishing on the Fraser. If you're trying to find an honourable way to end a relationship, or if you have some unfinished business in the heart department or any other place, a new country and a different work situation will not solve problems that you have neglected at home. Those sinister little triangular dynamics that hounded you in your personal or professional life are going to re-emerge like an untended rash, with potentially devastating consequences.

Ambiguity and disparity

In addition to the ebb and flow of your own emotions, and the emotions of those you need to care for as a partner or parent, you will be compelled to cope with an uncommon amount of ambiguity and disparity in your new life abroad. It will cause you no end of stress. You may have come to live a simple life with the poor and you find yourself lodged in a modest mansion, by your standards, with a maid, a gardener and a boy to clean the swimming pool. If you eventually have your way and rent a couple of rooms from a family in the townships, you still will have mountains more money and options than anyone around you. And now the family has to keep someone in the house day and night because neighbourhood thieves know a North American is living there.

Your lodging sorted out, what happens when your new work environment presents conditions that change the stakes for you completely? Maybe you've come from a Western church that ordains women; you've served three congregations already, and you now find yourself confronted with a senior male minister who points you in the direction of the Sunday school instead of the chancel? The solution is probably not to pack your bags before dawn, (it will confirm his suspicion that you are pampered and spoiled), nor is it necessarily to acquiesce and lie down as a six-month or three-year doormat. The only way to know how you chart a course in between those options is with a bit of wisdom and grace that may be quite outside of yourself.

Spiritual nurture

Some religious traditions place a great deal of emphasis on spiritual formation and the need to preserve quiet and space every day for prayer and ritual. Others have a strong worship component to their traditions but little sense that prayer can help direct their day-to-day activities. Regardless of where you place yourself on the continuum, you are entering a relationship with God and with God's people on this journey of a month or several years. It may be the only thing that helps you face the unexpected.

If you go to work overseas, though, even if it's only building latrines in the far-off rural reaches, and privately think that the people of faith there are naive or backwards in their search, you've attended the symphony and left during the tune-up. You will have missed a whole dimension of this overseas experience, in fact, the best part.

But a relationship is a relationship is a relationship—you have to work at it. Faith is confidence in God's tenderness, *especially* when we don't feel it. If you don't talk to God a lot, celebrate each other a lot, speak of your unfathomable love a lot, slam a few doors now and then (but not *too* hard) and share silly jokes that only the two of you will get, then you're also missing the best part. If you are new to this, there will be help in other chapters to get you started. Chances are you've known this faith language for many years, and belief is an integral part of your life. Nevertheless, it may be time for a second honeymoon.

If you think you need to close this book now and call off the wedding, then talk it over with someone you really trust before you catch the boat for the Fraser. Hopefully, this person's clarity has helped you see things in a new light in the past. If your suitcase is sitting on the bed half-packed and is still there by tomorrow at noon, we'll be with you on your journey in the months to come through this little book. Some of the things we'll talk about here will appear elaborated in future chapters. Some parts will be pure nuts and bolts suggestions of what you need to pack and unpack. Read what you need when you need it, but the next chapter will help you with some first steps so read it soon. We offer only suggestions in the pages that follow. Use what you find helpful, but leave room for the possibility that your experience may lead you to places and conclusions never imagined by the writers. It's just another measure of how wonderfully surprising faith ventures can be. The tune-up is over; the symphony is poised to play.

Exercise

Try this exercise with your family or a group of friends. Attempt to introduce yourself, communicate something about yourself, to someone else *without* using words.

How does it make you feel when you cannot communicate the simplest of phrases?

How important is it for you not to make a fool of yourself?

Do you tend to take on tasks that you've never done before even if you might do them badly and publicly, or do you need assurances before you set out that you will do this well?

What parts of communicating are most important to you?
> Having your ideas appreciated?
> Making others feel comfortable?
> Communicating acceptance?
> Being understood
> Other?

What are the implications for this across cultures?

How do you react when you cannot make yourself understood to a friend or loved one?

I want you to share your Bread with the hungry, open your homes to the homeless Poor, remove the yoke of injustice, Let the oppressed go free.

Isaiah: 58

2. Getting Ready

Islands of the north, east, west and south,
life on land and in the sea.
We are all creations of God's love,
meant to live in liberty.
We commit ourselves to peace today,
to be bold, to take risks, to try.
God be with us now and the days ahead
Hear our prayers, oh God, we cry.

> *by Lynda Katsuno, loosely based on poem by*
> *Alexandra Caverly-Lowry*

People who know themselves well and live comfortably in their own skins are often the ones who do best in cross cultural situations. The essence of the cross cultural exchange is not that you will do an historic piece of work, or that you will change the direction of any group or individual, or even that you will be of much use to anyone. Rather it's that sometimes those who are outside a situation have a different way of seeing things. If the outsider is reflective and a person of prayer, he or she might be able to offer some insight into situations that had been taken for granted, or that had baffled others to resolve.

This is not to be confused with the temptation to preface every conversation with, "At home we do it this way. ..." Most of us wouldn't have to go much farther than the length of a farmer's field to find a good dozen or so people in our lives who would tell us how to do everything better than we are currently doing it. The wise outsider does not jump in with quick solutions or pat answers. She or he cultivates humility, knowing that trust must be present for people to hear each other, and that trust must be earned. There also must be an underlying acknowledgement that the people of Tupelo have gotten along remarkably well in the past without your wisdom and ideas. The successful outsider goes as a learner, knowing full well that she or he will receive much more than can ever be returned in a month or three years.

If you have been chosen by your church for this assignment, you may already know the culture of your denomination inside out. In a sense, you speak the same language as those who hired you. Some denominations would not have considered you for overseas service if you sounded like a hot-headed revolutionary and others wouldn't have considered you if you hadn't displayed at least a bit of warm-headed activism. You share the same shades of theology: you express the same commitment to justice, you have an impelling personal spirituality, or perhaps you manage a balance of both. You may not walk on water, but there is no doubt that you tread it flamboyantly.

Many Canadian churches and secular groups that work for global justice have developed a language of intercultural relationships that involve important terms such as *"companions in mission"*, *"mutuality"* and *"partnership"*. While these concepts are important to understand and support, you need to be prepared for the possibility that they won't apply overseas in precisely the same way. While this cannot always be determined before you leave home, it's a good thing to anticipate that the church or organization that you are going to visit or work with will likely be more traditional than what you are accustomed to at home. But regardless of whether or not you encounter a theological difference, in many ways you will become a student of a culture within a culture. You will need to listen long and hard to understand this new culture as well as you understand your own. Often, the key may be to find discretion and composure in a situation that is twice removed from your own experience.

Nevertheless, you are on your way. You've been thinking about this for a long time. You and those who have accompanied you in this decision have tried to ensure that this is the best choice for you and those who will welcome you. And now that the assessing, self-assessing, discerning and interviewing are completed, all are convinced of your competence and that your desire, motives and commitment to work in Tupelo are sincere. You even feel a certain destiny to this - that you are called to it. Now, with a green light in your life, you will have to become very practical very quickly.

For the next little while you will have the growing sensation that you are straddling two horses going in different directions: you will be preparing yourself for the venture ahead while trying to tie up loose ends at home before you leave. If you have children and/or a partner to support as well, you'll have even less time to do your private leave-taking.

What to do - vaccinations and checkups

One of the first things you will need to do as soon as you know where you will be living overseas is to visit your family doctor or a travel clinic to determine which vaccinations you will need. Don't leave your shots until you're on the way to the airport; some vaccination series' can take eight weeks or longer to complete, and there is a chance that you won't be dancing for a day or two after some of them. A phone call to a travel clinic in your area will give you advice on the vaccinations that you will need. In some cases your doctor may advise you *not* to get a vaccination. Be sure to get a note with the doctor's reasons for avoiding the shots. (See Appendix C.)

It's essential for everyone to have a thorough checkup before you go overseas, and while you're at it, your family doctor can assure you that yours and your children's vaccinations and boosters are up-to-date. Diseases that are almost completely eradicated in the North are alive and thriving in other parts of the world.

Is there a doctor in the house?

In addition to the shots, a necessary unpleasantness, you will want to have a lengthy chat with your family physician about monitoring your health in a relatively isolated region. There is a great book produced by CUSO that you should take with you, it's called, *Staying Healthy While Overseas* (available from *The Canadian Churches' Forum for Global Ministries*. www.ccforum.ca). Others resource you may want to consider include *Where There Is No Doctor* and/or *Where Women Have No Doctor*, both available from Hesperian Foundation, www.hesperian.org. These illustrated manuals may be useful to you if you are in an isolated area and needing to monitor your own health, offering information about possible illnesses, signs, symptoms, and ways of caring for yourself.

Your doctor may suggest and prescribe some medications for you to have on hand for common illnesses: diarrhea, colds, nausea etc. You would likely not consider taking prescription medicines without seeing a physician at home, but in most situations overseas you will not be able to jump in the car and take yourself or a sick child to a 2:00 appointment across town. You also will want to talk to your doctor about putting together a basic medical kit. What goes into it will again depend upon location and the relative isolation of your work. In all likelihood in many countries of the world you will medicate yourself and your family through most illness, or, more importantly, you will learn the signs that tell you when to locate a doctor. If you don't know how isolated you might be, err on the side of caution and take the entire contents of the first aid kit mentioned in Appendix C. You will need a note (see sample in Appendix C) from your doctor indicating why you are carrying all these medicines and some needles. Appendix C also will give you a list of drugs you might consider taking. Talk to your doctor and he or she will instruct you on how to use them. Take notes! It's a long, long way to Tupelo, and you might not be in the state of mind to remember the exact medicating details, let alone the function, of the little green pills behind the thermometer four months from now.

Very often there will be someone in the area where you are going who treats the variety of common illnesses with herbs. Herbal cures can be a whole lot kinder to the body than prescription medicine, but slower to take effect. Herbal remedies are not for everyone, but try to keep an open mind about the wisdom of local healers and their knowledge of curative plants.

If you take prescription drugs, wear eye glasses, or a medic alert bracelet, obtain from your doctor a supply of the drugs and an extra pair of glasses and sunglasses. An additional bracelet is also a good idea. Make sure you purchase one that isn't flashy. As well, keep a copy of the generic name of the prescription drugs you are taking and the specifications of your lenses, in case you need to replace any of them while overseas.

Visas

This is as important as your ticket. You may be able to get a visa to work in Tupelo for the entire length of time you are overseas. On the other hand, your visa might be temporary and you will need to renew it from time to time by using some intricately incomprehensible way. As long as you have a visa to get into the country, you will be able to seek you guidance for whatever else is required later. You don't want visas to run out—bureaucrats are bureaucrats are bureaucrats in any country.

What to pack?

With any luck you will have heard from the person who is inviting you to Tupelo before you leave, but he or she may forget to tell you all the important things, like whether or not your hair dryer will work over there. That person can tell you about seasons which will give you clues about the clothing you should take. You might be expecting year-round tropical weather, to find that you are sweltering for four months of the year and freeeeeezing (with no indoor heating) the rest. Try to talk to people who have been to Tupelo to find out what kind of clothing is needed. As a general rule, natural fibers are best, cottons and woolens breathe better than polyesters. Unbleached cottons and high-luster polyesters provide good sun protection. Shirts or blouses with buttoned pockets can come in handy. In many places it is not acceptable for women and men to wear shorts, or for women to wear slacks or anything less than a blouse with sleeves. At a minimum, take comfortable walking/hiking shoes, flip-flops to wear in all showers— yes, some parasites can enter the body through bare feet—sturdy sandals and something you can dance in. In some climates leather will develop a blush of gray mold, so only take what wouldn't break your heart to lose. Your hat, your hat, don't forget your hat.

Obviously, the more simply you can live the better. But even in our desire to be pragmatic, thrifty and politically correct, we still need a bit of space for the odd instant cappuccino package, Bach, some special teas for high holy days, a silk shirt, as many inspired books as you can get away with, Neil Young, and the other small comforts that are personal if not eccentric.

Most airlines have serious restrictions on luggage, so you are best to pay attention to those limits or carry enough cash with you to pay for the extra. Remember if you change flights somewhere you might be required to pay again. Some rules of thumb apply:

- Never take anything that is of profound personal meaning for you. (Leave your late grandfather's gold bridgework with your parents or a close friend regardless of how much comfort it has brought you in the past.)

- Take valuable items like laptops, cameras, walkmans etc. in your carry-on luggage. Some things have a habit of getting lost when they are being transferred between flights in other countries. And try to explain that in halting Swahili.

- Tuck your passport and money as far away and as close to your skin as you can. Money belts are good. Pouches a bit bigger than your passport that go over your neck and rest under your shirt are more accessible and acceptable than undoing your zipper in the middle of the airport. Talk to your trip organizer or denominational contact to find out how much money you should take, then take a little extra. U.S. currency is generally the easiest to exchange anywhere. It's also a good idea to have a joint account with someone at home who is accessible, willing and able to send you money in a pinch.

- Take photos of your family and/or closest friends. If you want to live very simply overseas, take photos that do not display a lot of wealth at home. Photos will comfort you immensely, as well as give your new friends in Tupelo a sense of your tribe, something that will be very important to them.

- If you are a musician or have some kind of practical trade, like haircutting, take your instruments (anything less than a piano). These talents will sweep you into places and hearts faster than almost anything else.

- Set up a support network before you go. That sounds so simple, doesn't it? What you need to explain to your closest friends, however, is that they might be writing to you without much response for the six months or three years you are going to be away. The experience of most people is that they have energy to write to one or two people with some consistency for awhile, but then life and work get too complicated to explain in letters. Letters from home, though, are always treasured; your friends and family shouldn't stop writing because they don't hear from you. Ask them to trust you on this one.

- Symbols are very important as you take your leave. Stretch your imagination now and do something outrageously symbolic for those you are closest to: a locket for your mother; that Paper Bark Maple sapling your father really wants but won't break down and buy; reservations at a great restaurant nine months hence and leave the vouchers with your best friend (of course you can't make a reservation that far into the future, normally; talk to the manager.) You may be part of a blended family that will see adolescent or adult children staying behind at home. It will be important for you to set out a schedule of birthday and high holy day phone calls and send frequent and regular letters that your children can depend on. It will be very important for them to know that you have not forgotten them when you are apart. Try to arrange for them to visit you during their vacation. (To be on the safe side, if you are going to be working in a very remote area be aware that your desire to make a phone call on a particular hour or day may conflict with reality—the telephone workers went on strike; you had severe rains and the one telephone in the village six hours away is out—so assure your loved ones that if for some reason you don't get through, it won't be for lack of trying.)

When everyone looks back on your time away it will have flown by.

Looking ahead to six months or three years of significant loss without you, for them, can look interminable. You know what they say - it's harder to be left than to leave.

Personal well being

Taking care of your self at home is, to a certain extent, a personal decision. You can eat fast food and drink cherry colas until the cows come home. On the other hand, the likelihood of contracting something that will see your ears fall off as a result is far less than in some other countries of the world. That's not even mentioning the relative abundance of care in well-equipped hospitals to get you over an unexpected illness.

One of the most delightful ways people will share themselves with you in your new country is through food. You will want to acquaint yourself with all of their typical dishes and eventually learn to prepare them yourself. Food is not only at the heart of hospitality in most cultures, it is a way of opening ourselves and our homes to another, so there will be many times when you will know that it would be very offensive to refuse food or beverage. Eat with gusto and appreciation, and hope for the best. In your private time with your family, or as much as possible, you will need to be more careful than your local friends about what you eat. Living overseas carries some risks and this is one of them. Everyone has to decide how careful they want to be about living and eating "like everyone else". If you are going to be living in another country for three years you probably are going to reduce your vigilance somewhat about what you eat and drink. You will build up some tolerance over your time there, probably not without occasional bouts of diarrhea or illness.

Experience

One time we were running late and my companion and I were feeling very anxious to be back to a more secure location before nightfall. However, there was one more stop along the way at the home of the family of the pastor's wife to pick up their children who had been spending holidays there. Let's go in, pick them up and get out of here I thought. Of course, this was not possible; we had to hear all the news, greet the entire family and share a meal. In a tiny mud-smeared room we were served cornmeal porridge and tiny fish complete with heads, which no doubt had come out of the dubious looking ditch at the side of the house. My stomach was already turning because of my stress about the journey and I didn't know how I could do this. A silent prayer, a deep breath and a great gulp got me through it. Much later, the incident came back to me with great force when the pastor's wife said how impressed she had been that I had accepted to eat the food which I had been offered—that day, she said, she had come to think of me as one of them. **-RF**

If you are traveling or going for a short-term assignment six months to

18

a year, it is a good idea to be as vigilant as possible to avoid those beverages and foods that could cause you distress or illness, always keeping in mind that there will inevitably be occasions where you will need to compromise your standards. Most local people can eat foods prepared on the corner from street vendors without consequence, but it might incapacitate you for several weeks or require you to return home. Remember that you won't be of much help to anyone if you are sick for your entire visit; in fact you will probably be a considerable burden. Some people will think your habits fastidious, as you string your mosquito net in areas where malaria is prevalent, but the consequences of carelessness could follow you all the days of your life.

Experience
What almost made me change my mind about going to work in Nepal was hearing from a friend about his travels there, and his description of women nit-picking each other's hair. He assured me that catching lice was inevitable. I convinced myself that I should ignore him and went anyway. Little did I realize how casual I myself would become about the eventuality of head lice after it happened two or three times. It was a small price to pay for the joy of relating to Nepali villagers. -LB

Taking care to purify all the water you drink, (avoiding homemade drinks and drinks with ice); choosing fruits and vegetables that you can peel; only eating well-cooked meats that are served hot; avoiding mayonnaise and un-pasteurized milk products (including ice cream) will help considerably in keeping you healthy.

Sometimes local people or expatriates who have been living in Tupelo for years may forget that your body is vulnerable to the host of new bacteria in food and water, so it's up to you to take responsibility for your own health. Just because they can swim in the ocean that collects the city's untreated sewage doesn't mean you can. You could get very sick from foods and activities that their bodies have adjusted to long ago.

You need always to remind yourself when you are overseas that you are a guest and that your hosts have limited resources. They are already using a whack of them to have you there and to orient and train you. It's a responsibility for all of us to take as much care as we can to stay well and to avoid draining those resources more than is necessary.

Diarrhea
There will be times, riding a cantankerous bus climbing the mountains of Peru, when it's advisable to take medication that will stifle your diarrhea. It is recommended that you *always* carry your pills with you. In more familiar surroundings, that is, in your own home, it's worthwhile to allow the body's own good toxic waste disposal system to eliminate the troublesome food or beverage in its own time. Stop taking food and use electrolyte replacements or oral rehydration salts with purified water. Dehydration is the most common complication of diarrhea and

can usually be avoided if you remember to take one large glass of purified fluid after every bowel movement or when thirsty. Packets of oral rehydration salts can be purchased in many parts of the world. In North America they can be found under the name Gastrolyte and Pedialyte. Gradually you will be able to tolerate a little rice water, herbal tea, chicken soup if someone really loves you, or whatever local rejuvenating foods you hear mentioned by no less than five people. Avoid alcohol, fatty and spicy foods, caffeine and dairy products when you have diarrhea.

Sexual activity

You're going to get the sexual-relationships-overseas-are-not-a-good-idea talk further on in this booklet. Under this self-care section however, we're all being pragmatic. Things happen; far better that they be protected than unprotected things. Sexually active adults (or those hoping or intending to be) should take a good supply of condoms and spermicides.

You will need needles, syringes and condoms, of course, to prevent any diseases that are spread by blood, or body fluids, like semen. Mostly we're talking about *Acquired Immune Deficiency Syndrome* (AIDS), but you'd be surprised how often a bureaucrat wants to stick a needle into you to test for tuberculosis or some other mystery. And it's very hard to argue with a bureaucrat when you've only recently mastered, "Please, have you seen my luggage?" The numbers of cases of AIDS in Africa, Asia and Latin America is staggering. If you are in a motor vehicle accident or very sick, unless the situation is life-threatening, you will not want a blood transfusion overseas.

In case of emergency

Having given you enough reason in the preceding paragraphs to try out your diarrhea medication, chances are the worst you'll have to complain about in letters back to Canada are the fleas that have bonded profoundly only with you in your office. But there's a lot out there that's dangerous, not the least being cars, and this turning point in your life is probably as good a time as any to get your *Last Will and Testament* updated. Give some thought to the pros and cons of having a power of attorney or an enduring power of attorney established for someone at home. If you are going for more than six months you should definitely do this. At the very least, you should establish a bank account here with a co-signer.

Talk to your family and/or denomination about obtaining personal health insurance. It you choose to buy health insurance, or someone in your family wants to purchase it for you, be sure that it will cover overseas hospital bills. That's not automatic any longer, and provincial health budgets are stretched enough that, in most cases, provinces will accept no responsibility there either. You *must* keep all *detailed* bills and invoices related to illness, as well as a log of what treatments were performed. This could be important for your family doctor in the future.

Make three copies of all your documents—passports, visas, vaccination booklet, credit cards, travellers cheques, prescriptions, bank accounts. Give one copy to your tour guide, church or sending organization; leave one set at home with someone, and take a set with you. If you are going to be away for longer than a few weeks, prepare instructions, including funds, for what should happen in case of serious illness or death. Leave one set of the instructions in the care of someone at home and keep the other set with you. Obtain telephone and fax numbers for the person here who has the instructions and give them to your supervisor in Tupelo when it's appropriate.

Why wasn't I warned?

We've asked some people who have been through this, and others who have talked with or counselled them on their return, and they've come up with a list of the top things people wished they had been warned about before they left Canada. Many of these topics will be repeated in later chapters, but this is the one you're reading in preparation, so here goes:

Decisions: If you are going to work overseas, the local level is where you are going to have your greatest impact. At the structural level of the church or organization to which you are assigned, your opinion may not count for much. You may find that the important relationship is between your supervisor or someone even further removed over there and someone from your sending organization over here. Decisions may be made between them with little consultation with you, and you might not even be aware of what those decisions are. Experiencing the different levels of partnership between churches and organizations may take some getting used to. The people who are likely to feel this most are longer-term personnel.

Where do I go? The person who made the decision over there to have you come may have neglected to inform your future colleagues at the local level. When you get there you may discover that no one is really clear as to why you have come or what you are to do. You, in all of your newly arrived insecurity, may even pose a threat to some.

What do I do? Job descriptions, which are so important to us here in the North, may have very little importance in the particular overseas context in which you are going. Sometimes the only reason the overseas organization supplies a job description is to meet our need to have one, but it may turn out to have little relevance. The best advice may be to simply go with the flow until you are able to discern what is appropriate for you to be actually doing.

Partnership: You may go out confidently empowered by the ideas of partnership and accompaniment, but you may hear your organization or church referred to as a "donor agency."

Colonialism, alive and well: You are likely going to a country that was formerly colonized by another country. You may discover that the leaders there have adopted many of the same attitudes and actions of the former colonizers, which may tend toward the autocratic and hierarchical. While North American churches may wish to eschew the patterns of colonialism, there is a real danger that in the name of justice they can do the same thing, "We know what is really just in your situation, and we want to enlighten you."

Personal support: There may be much less support for you than you anticipated. You may be told that your primary support will be the responsibility of the overseas partner or organization. This may or may not materialize for a variety of reasons. People overseas may have a very different notion of support than you do, or the capacity of regional leaders to provide support may be very limited. Contact with your sponsoring organization, supervisor or church may be much less than you expected or wanted. That person may even be visiting in the country where you are living and not have time to see you. Also, people from home might not write as often as they hoped they could. It is important, therefore, to develop a support network among the people you are getting to know.

Well-being: You will need to take personal responsibility for your own learning and well-being. This includes developing those routines and rituals that will contribute to your spiritual nurture and development, your health care, and opportunities for recreation. You will need to know your own limits and recognize when you need to get away for awhile to take a break. Be aware of coping skills that will be important to you during what may be frustrating and personally trying times.

Racism: This is not something that only pertains to other people. You may discover racist or classist attitudes that you never thought you had. It may have been an undetected residue from your socialization. Try to find an old-time expatriate, someone who has lived in the country for many years and who has a profound love of the people there. This person will help you talk through your fears and prejudice, and enable you to see other sides of the people and the life. Also, you may want to be prepared to discover racist attitudes among some of the people you are going to visit or work with.

Pre-judging: Try to suspend judgement when you encounter a totally different situation than that to which you are accustomed. You may not need to decide what is right and wrong at this moment; in fact, moral judgments can sometimes prevent you from gaining new insights.

Convenience: Services and supplies we take for granted at home may not be present in the situation in which you find yourself. Telephone calls, communication and transportation can be major causes of frustration. Water back home is usually very plentiful and potable. Water where you are going may be scarce and contain very harmful bacteria. Electricity back home is readily available and is fairly constant, and our lifestyles seem to depend upon it to a great extent. In many other countries electricity may be scarce and intermittent. [Take along a flashlight and a battery recharger with appropriate adapters for differences in electrical currents.] You are probably not used to servants, nor do you wish to have any. In North America we tend to use appliances as our servants. But you may find that you need to employ someone as a domestic worker. Otherwise all of your recreation and rest time will be given to washing your clothing by hand and cleaning. If you do employ someone to help you and you make him or her feel very much part of your family, he or she may have hopes to return to your homeland with you. Seek advice on the local standard of remuneration, particularly for household help.

Safety standards: The standards that we take for granted at home may be very different overseas. You have to take more personal responsibility for your safety. Electrical appliances may be hazardous: you may, for example, encounter an electric water heater on the shower head of your bathroom. Transportation can present problems: the bus may often be grossly overloaded and people may be hanging out the doors as it is moving. Physical safety can sometimes be a problem. In many poor countries we are seen as wealthy people and are vulnerable to muggings and robbery. Only carry with you what you are prepared to lose.

Taxes: If you are going to be out of the country for a year or more, it is very important to find out about tax regulations at home and in the country to which you are going, particularly as they relate to residency. Make sure you clarify your residency status before going overseas. Ask your supervisor for some direction on this before you leave.

Who do I rely on? Don't assume that expatriates who have lived in the country to which you are assigned are always the best people from whom to get advice. Trust your best instincts and rely on nationals from your host country to guide you. In fact, get advice from everyone, and still expect to be wrong.

[With appreciation to George Lavery and Lorraine Reaume for these suggestions.]

Taking leave and looking forward

Jesus often called people away from what was familiar to them. But he always called them toward something, a new life, a different way of seeing the old. They left nets, riches, families, blindness and illness to be with him more intimately. Leaving, or being left, is a profound rupture to the human psyche. Some people never get over situations of loss that happen in their lives, so it is good to give a great deal of thought as to how you want to leave; how you will support your partner and children to leave, and how you will offer assurances to those who will miss you when you are gone. The story of the two disciples on the road to Emmaus is a story of grief and great hope. It confirms that Jesus will reveal himself to us on the journey in ways that only we will recognize. Sometimes we see him most clearly when we are in pain, when all of our senses need to see and hear him. Sometimes we hear him in the twilight after the pain has subsided a bit. But his promise remains that he will always be with us.

Luke 24:13-32: *That very day two of them were going to a village named Emmaus, about seven miles from Jerusalem, and talking with each other about all these things that had happened. While they were talking and discussing together, Jesus himself drew near and went with them. But their eyes were kept from recognizing him. And he said to them, "What is this conversation which you are holding with each other as you walk?" And they stood still, looking sad. Then one of them, named Cleopas, answered him, "Are you the only visitor to Jerusalem who does not know the things that have happened there in these days?" And he said to them, "What things?" And they said to him, "Concerning Jesus of Nazareth, who was a prophet mighty in deed and word before God and all the people, and how our chief priests and rulers delivered him up to be condemned to death, and crucified him. But we had hoped that he was the one to redeem Israel. Yes, and besides all this, it is now the third day since this happened. Moreover, some women of our company amazed us. They were at the tomb early in the morning and did not find his body; and they came back saying that they had even seen a vision of angels, who said that he was alive. Some of those who were with us went to the tomb, and found it just as the women had said; but him they did not see." And he said to them, "O foolish men, and slow of heart to believe all that the prophets have spoken! Was it not necessary that the Christ should suffer these things and enter into his glory? And beginning with Moses and all the prophets, he interpreted to them in all the scriptures the things concerning himself So they drew near to the village to which they were going. He appeared to be going further, but they constrained him, saying, "Stay with us, for it is toward evening and the day is now far spent." So he went in to stay with them. When he was at table with them, he took the bread and blessed, and broke it, and gave it to them. And their eyes were opened and they recognized him; and he vanished out of their sight. They said to each other, "Did not our hearts burn within us while he talked to us on the road, while he opened to us the scriptures?"*

Exercise

A check-list of things to do as I prepare to leave

Make a list of the people I want to take leave-of in a special way.

Block time in my schedule to do this unhurriedly.

Block time to talk to my partner/family, a friend, about leaving.

How can I /we help them feel a part of this venture and celebrate it with us?

How will I/we do this?

What /who will support me in my leaving?

How will I support my partner?

How will I /we help the children to leave well?

How do I/we help them articulate their fears?

What symbols can I use that will give them/me comfort when we're away?

What symbols will give those we leave behind comfort when we're away?

What arrangements have I made to ensure that there will be some contact with home?

I am among you as one who Serves

Lk:22

3   Getting There: First Things First

Our first task in approaching
> another people
> another culture
> another religion

is to take off our shoes
> for the place we are
> approaching is holy

else we may find ourselves
> treading on another's dream.

More serious still
> we may forget
> that God was there

before our arrival.[1]

In 1846, the Rev. John Geddie was summoned to the *Acadian*, a ship that would begin a journey of 18,000 miles from Halifax to the New Hebrides as Canada's first Presbyterian missionary to another country. Even though he was already a minister and had spent the year prior to his departure studying medicine, learning how to build boats, a printing press and set type, Geddie was not considered the perfect candidate, and controversy followed him almost to the moment he, his wife and two daughters boarded the ship that Sunday morning. He was considered too short, too sickly, too scantily trained in the classics. The list was long.

And if he were a man looking for signs he surely would have acknowledged some insecurity. The trip began with a compromise because the sudden shift of wind that would set them forth had taken place on the Lord's Day, and the first leg of the journey to Boston was an uninterrupted succession of storms. In his biography, *Missionary Life Among the Cannibals,* Geddie describes their leaving: "I went on deck to take a farewell look at Nova Scotia, and by the light of the moon I saw its blue mountains fast fading from view, far in the distance. When I remembered the many dear friends whom we had left behind us, and whose faces we should see no more in the flesh, I sighed; and I felt as if it would have given relief to my feelings to weep."

Out of the gates

It would be unusual if you were to arrive in Tupelo without a trace of mixed emotions. That trip of three months that took 19th century missionaries to exotic islands and dynasties on the other side of the world served the purpose of allowing the grief to subside and the psychological preparation to begin for what lay ahead.

You will have about 10 to 20 hours to do the same, so don't be surprised if you're feeling a little overwhelmed in the first couple of weeks. You'll probably need a lot of extra sleep at first, and you'll want

[1] Max Warren. From preface to *Sandals in the Mosque: Christian Presence Amid Islam.* Kenneth Cragg. New York: Oxford University Press. 1959. Used with permission.

to establish contact with home as soon as possible to tell them you're okay and offer your first impressions. This is as important for you as it will be for those you have left behind. (For those who are inclined, if you haven't already begun a journal this would be a good time to begin to put pen to paper.) You will also need to do some banking and your hosts will be helpful guides in understanding currency exchange.

Home away from home

At the very least your host should have arranged some temporary housing for you while you get settled, or this may be home for as long as you are there. On the other hand, you may be offered the option of looking for another place, but you will need some facility with the language and some friends (i.e. connections) to help you find what might eventually become home over the long term. Take your time, if you can. Many countries have very little to offer in mid-range accommodation since outside of North America and Europe the middle class shrinks dramatically.

There are always pros and cons to living under various conditions, and you are the only one who can decide what you personally can live with or without. The type of accommodation almost always has some correlation to the kind of experience of the country that you will take away with you. Sometimes the choice of accommodation will not be yours; your living situation is rustic, and you will learn to cope as best you can in a state that resembles permanent camping. Water and electricity will be a daily struggle, if they exist at all. In this environment there is no doubt that you will get to know local people in ways you otherwise never would. Seeing you standing in line at the lone water tap, the neighbourhood women will develop a very curious respect for your willingness to endure what they have no choice but to endure. You probably won't be near a telephone here and transportation will be a challenge.

In other situations, you will have a spectrum of housing arrangements to choose from. The following are stereotypes, of course; you will find lots of modification to these categories. They should provide a point of departure for you, though, to begin to think about your living arrangements.

Mercedes: This is the comfortable home with servants. It has a water tank on the roof for those times when there are shortages in your neighbourhood, and electricity is as constant as it gets anywhere. The house very often comes with a huge concrete fence all around it with broken glass jutting out of the top to dissuade those who might want to steal all the things they imagine you have behind those walls. This option might be closer to what you have come from, and the consequent experience of your host country will likely not be remarkably different from what you have left. Your goods will probably insulate you from the experience of the majority of people in the country.

28

Honda Accord: Nothing spectacular to look at, but reliable and practical. It comes with occasional help, someone to do the laundry and a clean-up once a month. It's not too secure so you might possibly lose your camera or IPod before you're through. Water in the house is more or less reliable and candles are in good supply for the nights when the electricity is out. Comfortable, not extravagant. Doors are open in this atmosphere and the world will come in. You will get to know your neighbours quite well, allowing a certain amount of privacy for you and your family, yet sharing in the daily struggles and celebrations of the neighbourhood.

Chevy Aveo: A room or two in someone else's home. This option injects a little money into the local economy. You will learn the language and customs faster because you are eating and sharing space with local people. You might not have as much privacy; it may be difficult to have guests, but you will gain in your understanding of the life of the Tupelese people, their struggles and fairly intimate family life. Your experience will be remarkably different from what you have left. This is a great idea for a short term.

Experience
Not only did we have the only latrine in the village, it was the best. The man who made it made it like a small house, so it was wonderfully large. The best thing was returning to that country nine years later to see almost every household with a latrine, not quite so grand but functional; it was very encouraging. LB

Considerations for single people
It seems to be a given in most cultures that a family requires privacy and space. Single people who are going for a longer term may need to be much clearer about their needs in this regard. Sometimes there is an expectation that single people must be lonely, so there is a relay of guests from early morning until late at night. There may also be an assumption that single people don't need the same accommodation or furnishings that a family would require, even though you have come to know and love a refrigerator and stove in your other life. Sometimes single people are requested by overseas partners or churches, with the expectation that they will live happily in a single room with a hot plate. If your host organization is responsible for your housing, you may need to negotiate very early on what you can live with and without. Obviously you cannot demand running water in the house if the entire population of the township uses one water tap down the street, but you do need to cook, so a stove and possibly a refrigerator are not out of the question in most circumstances.

To work and back
Transportation follows housing in that if you choose to own or lease a car it will insulate you one more layer from local people. Generalizations are not very helpful, here, because your work or travel may find you in Tokyo, where housing and transportation are state of the art.

But most travel and work overseas is in countries where public transportation is unreliable. In some cases, Murphy's law of transportation applies in exaggerated forms: if you are in a hurry, you will accidentally catch the bus that takes you to the centre of the city, 45 minutes away from your destination and you will have to pay $10 to get a taxi back; if you are feeling a little queasy, the bus will break down beside the outdoor fish market at 4:00 in the afternoon of the hottest day of the year. You may be pick-pocketed, and, if you are a woman, you may be subjected to a variety of forms of sexual harassment in the crush of city buses. If you like order, you will be amazed at how religiously people form a line-up until the bus door opens, and then break the line with all the instincts of basic survival, leaving mostly the women and children to re-form the line-up and wait for the next bus.

Experience

We were in Lusaka for a meeting which went longer than anticipated, and by the time we got to the central bus stop, the crossroad was teeming with people anxious to get home after the working day. The sun was dropping fast, adding to everyone's anxiety. Bus after bus pulled in, but each time a gang of young men took over, whacking would-be passengers, and letting through friends and those prepared to pay them a commission. Women with small children were afraid to press forward and only got on the bus by fluke. We were offered a chance to pay to be put forward, but we hung back secure with the knowledge that we could always afford a taxi to our accommodation. The red sun ball set long before we got a seat on a bus. -**LB**

At other times you will be moved to witness spontaneous acts of kindness among the bus travellers who are all tired and, like you, doing their best to survive. It may be customary for those seated to take the parcels of those standing. On a day when your last ounce of inner fuel is spent someone unexpectedly offers you a seat. An older woman, at some personal cost, alerts you to the pick-pockets with winks and nudges. Even though they'll have to wait another half hour for the next bus, some men step down and let the women and children board first.

Experience

My work in Nepal was in a rural area so hilly that there were no roads suited for cars. On one occasion, a couple of teenage boys accompanied me into the city, a walk of about 10 hours before we hit a road. I was keen to take whatever transport was available. A taxi came along and we got in. It was the boys' first ride in a motor vehicle, and I had a real belly laugh, especially when we reached our destination and had trouble opening the door; the boys scrambled out the window. I guess that's how I often looked to them in my ignorance of how things were done in the village. We learned a lot from one another. –**LB**

Market techniques

Once you have a roof over your head, you will need to buy some provisions. It would be best to find a local person who is willing to take you on his or her regular shopping trip to the market. You can get to know the vendors he or she uses and they will treat you fairly. In some situations you are expected to barter and that takes a bit of facility with the language but not much; a well-timed frown can sometimes go a long way, even if you didn't quite understand what was said to you. Try to learn prices, listen to people in the line-up before you and expect that you might be overcharged a bit, because you look like you can afford it. Many markets have a two or three-tiered pricing system. Expect it, and learn to avoid outrageous rip-offs.

Be particularly careful about the purchase of meat and milk overseas; patronizing vendors who are used regularly by the people you work with is a good way to go. Ask someone to teach you about the foods that are unfamiliar to you. If you were raised on the prairies, ask someone to show you how to buy fresh fish; find out how to choose good local fruit in season. You may not get your supervisor's help, but there will be some local people who will be able to give you a bit of time as you get yourself established, and they will be happy to be asked. Be a bit careful not to take up too much time of any one person. You may find that some of the people you find most interesting have virtually no time to spend with you: they work a second job; have four children at home; get up at five o'clock to prepare the day's food; wash for the entire family on the weekend, iron and sew in the evenings.

Language barrier

With any luck you will be given a few weeks to several months to learn the Tupelese language if it is different from your own. Nothing will bruise your self-confidence more than a three year old with perfect capacity to speak and be understood, who turns away from you, after trying to make you understand something, muttering, "Wow you're stupid," which you understood *all* too well.

The nuances of some languages, far from the romance tradition, will not be learned in 10 years. Others will be understood within six months to a year. You will always begin to comprehend far sooner than you will be able to reply with much fluency That becomes particularly difficult at the level of feelings. The ability to express what you are feeling with any subtlety is very slow in coming and there is going to be a long stretch in which you are going to feel entrapped because you cannot express yourself.

Experience

It seemed like there were all kinds of things going on that I was oblivious to; they're subtleties that you're just not aware of. It's not lack of language. There are certain rules of the culture or ways of being that you just don't know. For example, there was a gathering for a first birthday party in my neighbourhood, and afterwards the adults sat around and drank. The couple I lived with also went. After the party, my friend Carmen said to me, "How you said that, or how you did that, that was wrong; you made people feel uncomfortable because of that." She explained it to me three or four times, and I still didn't understand. I couldn't figure out what I had said to make people feel uncomfortable. It was so frustrating because I would never want to do that. -LR

Sometimes, because the struggle to learn and communicate is so hard and draining, the temptation is to gravitate toward the expatriate community for your sole support. They will be excited to admit some new blood into their circle and you will be relieved to find people who understand your bad jokes. Without a doubt there is a time to be with your own people, but there are some drawbacks to spending too much of your leisure time with other foreigners, not the least of which is the message it gives to your Tupelese colleagues who cannot afford pizza on Friday nights, or tennis and swimming at The Club.

After the formal language study has finished, try to find a local teacher whom you could pay to continue your lessons or help you purchase books that would expand your vocabulary. Obtaining some help reading the newspaper is also a good way to improve your fluency, as is watching television: these will allow you to keep in touch with the world, and will enable your teacher to expound on national politics, international affairs and local scandals.

Culture on the rocks

Learning another culture is five degrees removed from the language. It requires patience and a kind of looking and sensitivity that most of us, accustomed to hearing our prompts, are not versed in. Some cultures will be close to your own and will make light of your cultural gaffes, provided you learn from them.

Expectations revolve mainly around clothing and behaviour. The roles of men and women, for instance, are most often clearly delineated. You may cause some stir if you are a happily single person, or a childless couple with no desire to have babies for awhile. Women chat with women in the kitchen at a party and men sit around and talk among themselves.

Experience
You learn a lot very fast by making mistakes. The first day I was there, I was at the head office of the national church. There were about seven people there, all male and all older than I was. I was being my jovial self and joking with them. That evening I got a list presented to me, written in English, of the people with whom it was appropriate to joke. I, as a young woman, had broken *all* the rules. -MD

In another culture, no clues of your transgressions will be offered and everyone will be so gracious as never to say *no* to you, even though you may be making a wildly outrageous request by their standards. Your wish to photograph a den of lions will just never materialize— the car breaks down, cousin Mbuto's mother is sick, it's too hot.

In other cultures still, you will learn to anticipate any number of responses to your request and offer ways of allowing your hosts to "save face" if it is a no that they must deliver to you. Failure, as in failing to please you, is a serious humiliation in some cultures. You will learn to offer an "out" that will appear to be even better than what you truly wanted, or you will learn to ask your questions through a third party. It's a very formal dance.

Experience
In my English class of 50 Junior High girls at a Christian School in Tokyo, all of whom were as silent as possible, I realized that one girl, when forced to speak, sounded like a native speaker of English. After the class I spoke to her, and she reluctantly told me that her father was a diplomat and she had attended school in England for some years. I thought she was wasting her time in this very basic class and that she should be encouraged to train as an English teacher herself. I spoke to the head of the English department in this regard. The following week, I discovered that she had been removed from the class and was spending that hour in the library. All I succeeded in doing was to embarrass her by bringing her to the attention of her classmates and separating her from them. I should have known that in Japan all students— mediocre, average or exceptional—stay with their age group throughout their school year. -MP

Most often you can find a kindly person who begins to look out for you and will gladly take you under a wing and explain some customs to you. You have a lot to learn, so keep going back. That person will also give you a lesson on all the naughty words if you ask, which is very useful especially when it's easy to pick up phrases without benefit of translation. This friend will also give you hints about appropriate clothing that you should agree to wear in your public time.

Fitting in
If you've ever stood helplessly outside the fence to the school playground as your little eight year-old is pushed away by three other little girls who hold hands firmly in a circle in order to keep her out, you will recall with sadness how profound is our need to fit in, whatever our age. Single people look longingly to couples who are overseas because at least they have each other. Couples look back at single people because they seem to integrate themselves more quickly, and the loneliness can seem worse when you're with someone but feel completely unsupported. Parents want their children to benefit from the overseas experience, not end up emotionally scarred by it. Fitting in just takes time; it's as simple and hard as that.
Experience

I was going to be away for a few days and told the family I was living with that I would not be back until late at night on Tuesday Circumstances changed, and I ended up coming back earlier than expected, right in the middle of a special meal, with relatives and guests over, but I was met with a wonderful surprise. The moment I stepped through the door, they said, "Come, sit down, we already set a place for you at the table. We said to ourselves, "We know she will be thinking of us while she is away, so we wanted to remember you by having a place for you." I was profoundly touched and grateful. **-LR**

Your hosts will provide opportunities to gather with people, and a congregation or parish is another likely place to meet those who share your values and might become your friends. It may turn out that you never find anyone who matches the kinds and quality of relationships that you've known in the past. It's still worth it to get to know a few people and their lives and struggles, no matter how different you might feel from them. Sometimes it is surprising how remarkably similar experiences and human nature are, even across cultures, and, who knows, you might find a kindred spirit among the people of this new land who makes the culture and language almost disappear, and you know that the mutual quality of the friendship will keep the two of you close for the rest of your days.

Experience

The friendships and relationships with local people were, of course, very important, and my whole reason for being there. When it came to those friendships where I felt a strong connection in terms of truly being known and understood, however, with one exception, the bonds were stronger with a few other North American missionaries. This is not to place a value judgment on any of these relationships. I believe it is important to recognize and appreciate the differences that are there. For example, one woman I visited a lot was about my age. There most similarities stopped. She had a husband and five children, while I am single; she could not read or write; I had been able to visit more of her country than she had; she made her living selling the leftover parts of chickens; she was an expert folkloric dancer; she intuitively knew things from her ancestors which she could not articulate, but which gave her a wisdom and an ability to cope with extreme hardship. It was wonderful to know her, to be with her in times of struggle in her family, and to dance with her at times of celebration. But our worlds, our entire life experiences, were very different. We enriched each other, but there were many things we would never truly understand about the other, simply because we had lived completely different lives. I feel it's important to appreciate these differences for two reasons: one, so as not to minimize the complexity of each individual life and, two, so new or shorter term visitors do not put undue pressure on themselves, or those receiving them, if they do not feel they are making lots of close friendships with local people like they are "supposed to". The effort to connect and have relationships is necessary and good, but I think true and deep friendships are a gift of God. **-LR**

Relationships—whether they are new and awakening, or long-time, rich and comforting—are always a mystery. Does he remind me of someone? Do her ideas resound inside me in a delightful way? Am I attracted to the way he has of acknowledging people with care; the way she throws back her head and laughs from her belly? Do I wish I could celebrate life the way they do? When it's working really well, we don't usually analyze a relationship. We indulge in it. And rightly so.

If you are the kind of person who can find in yourself a willingness to appreciate difference—different ways of being, different habits, different opinions—you will likely make friends with ease in this new culture. If you like the parts of yourself that are different, you will most likely be willing to embrace them in someone else. If you make friends easily in general, our guess is that you'll do swimmingly in Tupelo. These are hints followed by guesses.

Experience
There was a village wedding and all were invited. The family, where I was living, took a look at me and the mother said, "It's time for you to change into something else." I felt wonderfully accepted that she felt that free to help me know what I should wear. **-LB**

Choosing a lifestyle
Throughout the New Testament, Jesus is calling us beyond where we are, always beyond. Crossing boundaries of faith is a daunting and frightening experience. Making decisions about your lifestyle will have implications for the authenticity of your work in another country. Here are some passages to think about as you decide how you are going to live in this new country.

Luke 12:22-34
And he said to his disciples, "Therefore I tell you, do not be anxious about your life, what you shall eat, nor about your body, what you shall put on. Tor life is more than food, and the body more than clothing. Consider the ravens: they neither sow nor reap, they have neither storehouse nor barn, and yet God feeds them. Of how much more value are you than the birds! And which of you by being anxious can add a cubit to your span of life? If then you are not able to do as small a thing as that, why are you anxious about the rest? Consider the lilies, how they grow; they neither toil nor spin; yet I tell you, even Solomon in all his glory was not arrayed like one of these. But if God so clothes the grass which is alive in the field today and tomorrow is thrown into the oven, how much more will God clothe you, O people of little faith! And do not seek what you are to eat and what you are to drink, nor be of anxious mind. Tor all the nations of the world seek these things; and your God knows that you need them. Instead, seek God's kingdom, and these things shall be yours as well.

Luke 19:1-9

He entered Jericho and was passing through. And there was a man named Za-cchaeus; he was a chief tax collector, and rich. And he sought to see who Jesus was, but could not, on account of the crowd, because he was small of stature. So he ran on ahead and climbed up into a sycamore tree to see him, for he was to pass that way. And when Jesus came to the place, he looked up and said to him, "Zacchaeus, make haste and come down; for I must stay at your house today." So he made haste and came down, and received him joyfully. And when they saw it they all murmured, "He has gone in to be the guest of a man who is a sinner." And Zacchaeus stood and said to the Lord, "Behold, Lord, the half of my goods I give to the poor; and if I have defrauded any one of any-thing, I restore it fourfold." And Jesus said to him, "Today salvation has come to this house."

Exercise

How do these passages speak to me about how God is calling me be-yond where I am right now?

How do they reflect my need to plan and prepare for the future?

What do they say to me about my need for material goods?

How do I, as a parent, act with faith yet care responsibly for my fam-ily?

What are the implications of living:
> in a wealthy home with servants,
> in a modest home with some help,
> like the people I have come to work with.
> in right relationships.

How authentic is it for me to live like the people if I am in essence much wealthier?

How will people view my desire to live like them, or to live differently than they do?

4 Journeying in the Spirit

If you've ever seen parents send off a teenager for a night out with friends and the car, you'll know it goes something like this: don't forget your seat belt; don't drive above 40; don't pass anyone, don't turn the radio on, it'll distract you; don't smoke; don't scratch; don't look at anybody; don't talk to anybody; don't sneeze, don't be later than midnight; don't. . .and the very last command as the harried young adult slinks out the door is, "Oh, and have a good time."

Lest we forget to say it to you, in the rush of warnings and worries, have an outrageously wonderful time! You are beginning one of the most exhilarating, mind and spirit-altering adventures of your entire life. When your grandchildren ask you to stretch back and look at those profound experiences of your life, this will be among the ones you include.

It won't be because you are going away; every day people travel to different parts of the world and get to know other cultures and peoples. This marvelous journey is much more than an excursion or cruise. It is a quest, a journey of your spirit. You have a kind of assurance that others do not. You have the assurance that you are doing what you believe to be God's will for you right now. At this moment in your life, to the best of your understanding, you are in the right place at the right time. There is an incredible grace in knowing that. Jesus says, *"if you want that mountain to move and you believe it is already done, it will be so."* That's the promise to his followers.

Over and over again, the scriptures promise God's blessing and abundance if we seek and do God's will with earnestness.

Is not this what I require of you?
to loose the fetters of injustice,
to untie the knots of the yoke,
to snap every yoke
and set free those who have been crushed?
Is it not sharing your food with the hungry,
taking the homeless poor into your house,
clothing the naked when you meet them
and never evading a duty to your kinfolk?
Then shall your light break forth like the dawn
and soon you will grow healthy like a wound newly healed;
your own righteousness shall be your vanguard
and the glory of the Lord your rearguard.
Then if you call, the Lord will answer;
if you cry to the Lord, the Lord will say,
"Here I am. . . .
if you feed the hungry from your own plenty
and satisfy the needs of the wretched,
then your light will rise like dawn out of darkness
and your dusk be like noonday;

the Lord will be your guide continually
and will satisfy your needs in the shimmering heat;
God will give you strength of limb; you will be like
a well-watered garden like a spring whose waters
never fail. The ancient ruins will be restored by
your own kindred and you will build once more on
ancestral foundations;
you shall be called Rebuilder of broken walls,
Restorer of houses in ruins.
Isaiah 58: 5-12

You could see this journey as an opportunity to come to know Jesus of
Nazareth in new ways. Begin as if he had just entered the room. Someone whispers to you that this person will influence you like no one
else you've met in your entire life. Go back to the stories of him in the
New Testament. Read them, savour them, imagine being present in all
of them. To what does he call you? Who are you by the Sea of Galilee?
With the woman caught in adultery? Who are you during the trans-
figuration? At his arrest? Begin your relationship with Jesus all over
again. Talk to your partner about him. Make time to study and pray
every day. Allow the insights of this relationship to inform your work,
your life, your partnership, your time with your children. Tell them
the stories. Listen to their questions.

There is another way that you can come to know Jesus during this
time—through the people you have come to visit or serve. This, oddly,
will represent a kind of transformation for you too. It may seem initially that your experience is so far removed from these people that
there can be no real meeting-ground. Eventually, though, you will begin
to see beyond the roles, beyond the obstacles, the culture; you may even
begin to see wisdom in doing things in different ways, their way. You
may come in with an attitude and ambition to change things for the
better, and find *yourself* being changed, converted, for the better.

Experience
About a year before I went, a lot of the old images of God started
falling away for me, so I was left going overseas without any
image of God; it was a bit tough then. I remember during language school that I felt as if everything had fallen away. It was
one of those dark nights of the soul times—and there were a few
of those—where you're just praying and feeling like you're not
connecting. I think the faith of the local people helped me. It was-
n't my own expression of faith, but the intensity of their faith and
the depth of it really touched me—that under such horrible circumstances they continued and believed and had faith. I didn't
feel that it needed to be my faith, but it was the same God they
were connecting with. It was just so obvious that God was *with*
people in the most horrible, painful circumstances, then I thought
God must be there for me too in some way. **–LR**

In the book, *One Christ—Many Religions: Toward a Revised Christology,* author S.J. Samartha describes two kinds of Christology that also offer insight into the way we communicate our understandings in another culture.

"Among many Christians, there seems to be a desperate need to defend and guard the divinity of Christ, lest by starting from below one might compromise the confession that 'Jesus is the Christ, son of the living God.' Is this fear historically and theologically justified? A *helicopter* Christology, in its attempts to land on the religiously plural terrain of Asia, makes such a lot of missiological noise and kicks up so much theological dust that people around it are prevented from hearing the voice and seeing the vision of the descending divinity. A bullock-cart Christology, on the other hand, always has its wheels touching the unpaved roads of Asia, for without continual friction with the ground, the cart cannot move forward at all. Moreover, a bullock-cart Christology has the advantage of having its bullocks move on with a steady pace, even when the driver sometimes falls asleep."

(One Christ - Many Religions: Toward a Revised Christology, by S. J. Samartha © Orbis Books, Maryknoll, New York 10545. Used with permission.)

There are so many ways in which we have acted as helicopters when entering a new culture, because most of us have been conditioned to assume that difference is slightly inferior. If you take the slow road in, however, getting to know people by sight, working with them, acknowledging them in their struggles, or just sitting with them in the dust, you will learn so much more about those you are coming to know, about yourself and God.

It took a long time for the churches to acknowledge this, but by the 1960s, respect for other Christians and other faiths was emanating from many denominations. At the levels of their leadership, at least, Christian denominations were down-playing the need to save souls from damnation. When the debate finally subsided, it was clear that Christians were still needed to bear witness to the mystery of Christ, says Mary Motte when describing the Roman Catholic experience in this area. In *Toward the 21st Century in Christian Mission,* she describes what she calls the "dialogue of life" approach to mission.

"Dialogue of life is described as the 'daily practice of brotherhood [sisterhood], helpfulness, openheartedness and hospitality,' and joint commitment to 'whatever leads to unity, love, truth, justice and peace' *(Federation of Asian Bishops' Conferences, #49, 1987.)* This way of understanding sees dialogue as a lifestyle that entails 'living in harmony with people of other faiths, forming an open attitude toward other religions, sharing religious experiences and working together with peoples of other faiths.'"

(From *Roman Catholic Missions* by Mary Motte, F.M.M., in *Toward the 21st Century in Christian Mission,* edited by James M. Phillips and Robert T. Coote, Wm. B. Eerdmans Publishing Co., ©1993. Used with permission)

Experience
My work was in a fairly remote rural community. I had to do a lot of walking, sometimes six or eight hours at a stretch. On one such day, I had run out of water and stopped by a farm house to ask for a drink. At first the woman turned down my request, saying they had no water. But I knew they did; our project had installed the water pipe. When I asked again, she explained that they were of a low caste. I told her I would drink her water. She was amazed. It made me think of that passage where Jesus asked for water from the woman at the well. -LB

That you will find yourself and your faith stretched in ways you never imagined is not surprising. But there is another side to the transformation that goes beyond your personal self-understanding. The longer you work in a country where poverty is the norm, the more questions will arise within yourself. You will ask yourself, "What's wrong with this picture?" You will begin to notice the disturbing inequities and injustices close to you: a neighbour's child is diagnosed with tuberculosis; a co-worker's son is beaten for talking about a union in the factory where he works. You begin to wonder why people must live in misery; why your friends have to hold down two jobs just to make ends meet; why the majority of the people of the country have access to such limited resources; why people are chronically underemployed; why medicine costs so much; why farmers use their fields to grow crops for export rather than food for their families; why countries are obliged to pay off crippling debts owed to wealthy countries at the expense of health care and literacy for their own people. Then you will begin to analyze some of the economic and political structures within the world that rely on a pool of cheap, non-unionized labour in poor countries to make a profit. You will begin to notice that pesticides long-ago banned back home are used in abundance in poor countries. You will see companies, whose logos are familiar to you, polluting the lakes and rivers of countries too poor to say no to foreign investment. You may already have known all this, as knowledge, when you lived in the North; now it means the health and welfare of people you have lived with and care for.

And when you have arrived at that place, you will discover for yourself a new mission. You will, someday sooner or later, need to return to your own country and talk about your experience as well as you can. Only the same rules apply: if you come back like a helicopter, people aren't going to hear you. If you come back, as a bullock cart, finding them where they are, taking seriously their struggles and pain, treating them as human beings doing their best, but seeing differently, you will more likely gain their trust and affection and thereby affect change in them in the long run. They will see you as mellowed, wise even, more humble, not rabid and judgmental, a listener of the heart. And they will be compelled to hear your words

A spirituality to sustain you[2]

A spirituality of global mission links us to the many concerns and issues that are daily faced and fought by our brothers and sisters the world over. We look to see the face of Jesus in others, and when we really see Jesus there we begin to care about their welfare. Their struggles become our struggles. Through compassion and solidarity we become united in mind, heart and purpose. It is the Spirit who teaches us, and it is the Spirit that reveals to us more and more of what it is to be one with God. The closer we are to God, the closer we are to others, and vice versa. This is, in practical terms, how we become a people of God; this is how we build up the body that is Christ. In this way our spirituality draws us closer to one another, makes us one; and the more this happens in us, the more we become part of that body; we become Eucharist to one another.

The face of poverty reveals to us a face of Jesus that many in our day would prefer not to look at. Yet our mission is to see Jesus especially in the crucified of our world, the victims of injustice, the stranger, the outcast, the demoralized and abused. If the Spirit is with us, we will move towards others in compassion and love, with a passion for justice and a desire to build authentic community. Those whom the world rejects will be our friends. Our fellowship is with the lowly and those who hunger for God and the reign of justice: victims of violence and torture, the poor, and so many others. Perhaps we cannot be friends to all, but we are part of a much larger body that can reach further than we might imagine or hope for. If we do our part for the body, we are accomplishing our mission and building up the whole.

This form of justice spirituality is able to work particularly well when we realize that it is the power of God within us that makes this possible. We are not sufficient within ourselves to bring about the revolutionary realization of the "kingdom" that Jesus described in the scriptures as God's own plan for all creation. As we reach out to others in solidarity, we recognize this more and more; we are able to celebrate the power of the Spirit to do more than we could ever imagine, the Spirit that works in nature, in other religions, in other lands.

There are elements that we will never understand about another's world or culture because it is distinctly their own. This is not surprising, or even problematic, for those committed to the kind of mission spirituality we are discussing here. There is always more to learn and more to do. Those we love most, those we call friends, those we try to serve in our ministry, these are the ones who invariably teach us most. Mission is an ongoing process of reaching out and receiving, of meeting God in others in new and surprising ways.

For this to take place, we must recognize our own limitations while at the same time making the leap of faith that all is possible through and with the Spirit. Our spirituality is the life blood of our faith; it nourishes and sustains us in ministry and helps us to understand the meaning of our daily struggles within a rooted context, a context that is one of

[2] Kevin Anderson. *Canadian Churches' Forum for Global Ministries.* 1995. Used with permission.

41

many contexts throughout the world. It is the Spirit that builds the bridges between these contexts. It is the Spirit active in others that causes us to change our perceptions and attitudes, that leads us to new ways of feeling, thinking and acting. And finally it is the Spirit that teaches us, that reveals we are connected to all that is in the universe.

Exercise

- How does my prayer life sustain me in my present life and how do I expect it to support me in mission?

- How would I articulate a spirituality of mission?

- What are the reasons that I feel called to this work and this experience?

- What do I expect to learn from the Spirit?

- What do I expect the Spirit to do in me? To ask of me? To call me toward and beyond?

I will Love those called "unLoved" says God... who raises the Lowly and fills the hungry with good things.

Hs, 2, Lk. 1

43

5 Support Groups

Indian Tapestry

When I go up to the house of the Old Weaver
I watch in admiration
what comes forth from her mind:
a thousand designs being created
and not a single model from which to copy
the marvelous cloth
with which she will dress
the Companion of the True and Faithful One.

Men always ask me
to give the name of the label,
to specify the maker of the design.
But the Weaver cannot be pinned down
by designs,
nor patterns.
All of her weavings
are originals,
and there are no repeated patterns.
Her mind is beyond all foresight.
Her able hands do not accept patterns or models.
Whatever comes forth, comes forth,
but she Who Is will make it.

The colours of her threads
are firm:
blood,
sweat,
perseverance,
tears,
struggle,
and hope.
Colours that do not fade
with time.

The children of the children
of our children
will recognize the seal
of the Old Weaver.
Maybe then
it will be named.
But as a model,
it can never again
be repeated.

Each morning I have seen
how her agile fingers
choose the threads
one by one.

Her loom makes no noise,
and men
give it no importance,
and nevertheless,
the design
that emerges from Her Mind
hour after hour
will appear in threads
of many colours
in figures and symbols
which no one, ever again,
will be able to erase
or undo.

By Julia Esquivel from *Threatened with Resurrection*, 2nd edition. © 1994 Brethren Press, Elgin, IL 60120. Used with permission.

Finding the right level of support for your self in Tupelo is akin to crafting mortise and tenon corners on a drawer for an old dresser. You chisel and sand until you think you've got it—too little chiselling and it will swell in damp weather and split; too much and cabinet-maker's glue will not hold it. At the least bit of stress it will give away.

For some people, accompaniment is an intimate party with their closest 40 friends. They are renewed in a crowd, manage to stay engaged in the detail of the lives of dozens of people, nurture those relationships with a full calendar of visits and calls, and stay on top of a thriving correspondence with two dozen more besides. You would think that support would follow this person, and it won't take long, but the first few months without that vast array of contact could even challenge the most extroverted of extroverts.

For the more introverted, the process is clearer; cultivating support is a deliberate activity with a small group of people. You walk a fine line between engaging with people in work or leisure and needing to withdraw from the crowd for renewal. Too much socializing cuts into the time left for your real kind of rejuvenation. Support comes from a handful of close friends and, in the perfect world, they would be people who know you, your tribe and loyalties, who sympathize with your values and beliefs, understand your work and have some investment in you. But more than all of this, they need to be people who can be honest with you, even when the truth is unpleasant.

In Tupelo, set adrift from those friends who have shared history with you, you'll begin to search for the kind of support you need to keep yourself nurtured and grounded in your new experience. While it's a good idea to search for a small group for connection, there is as much grace as good management sometimes when it comes to finding exactly what you need. You may have a dozen structures set up at work and in your community to provide support for you; expatriates falling over themselves to keep you company, and you find what nourishes your soul is a small Mayan youth group from the next village learning the ancient dyeing and weaving techniques of their ancestors. Don't be surprised if it comes from where you least expect it.

If you have come to Tupelo with a partner or as a family, you may feel that you are a self-sufficient unit with enough support; or you may feel that you have too much on your mind running a household and helping the children adjust to their new environment to worry about your own support. While it is true that you have a great deal to cope with, sometimes the partner who does not have the identified outside work spends so much time caretaking in the first few months that he, or more often she, suddenly is far behind in personal adjustment to the new culture. Your children are already bubbling with the language; your spouse is making friends and coping well with work, and you have been left six strokes behind in language training and adaptation. If you are going to be isolated, (and that can just as easily be in the midst of a five-member family,) be sure to find a way to stay connected with the world beyond your home, even if it's to have tea with other people in a similar situation once a week.

How/Where do you find friendship?

It is always worthwhile to check in with your congregation or parish. There may be Christian community groups that have formed that you could join. In a congregation you have a good chance of finding like-minded people who share your values and understand your symbols. This may not be what you had in mind as personal support, but it will enable you to get to know more people, and invest in local support down the road.

> **Experience**
> A woman came to my house one day, saying that she had a problem because a friend of a friend's daughter was getting married and she was responsible for making the wedding cake. She'd never made a cake before. So she came to me to say, "Can you teach me how to bake a cake? I've got everything here that we need." She had nine eggs, some flour, some sugar and some yeast. So I said, "let's make a cake." Over an open fire we put the ingredients together and I substituted some baking powder for yeast and we made this cake. She couldn't speak English and I couldn't speak Swahili, but we had enough to communicate what we needed to. -MD

For a time, your support might come from the expatriate community—other Christians working for denominations overseas or people working for humanitarian causes. With them you will, at least, have your first language in common and be able to freely verbalize your impressions of your new situation to someone who has been through the transition. You could not speak as freely about the things that annoy you initially about Tupelo or what you miss about home with your Tupelese friends.

Secondly, find a couple of people you connect with and plan to visit on a regular basis, every two or four weeks. You might structure your time around something you have read, but its probably better to keep the gathering as free of preparation as possible, otherwise you might begin to resent the time involved. Sharing food is a good way of creating community and opening hearts, and since everyone has to eat every day, there isn't the weight of a great deal of extra preparation involved. Keep these occasions as simple as possible, so that attention can be given to each person as they relate their feelings and events since the last get together.

Spiritual companions

Finding a couple of people to share friendship with *as well as* your faith perspective is even better than time together to share language and travel catastrophe stories, but these folk may be harder to come by Some religious communities have a tradition of spiritual direction. A person who is wise in experience and human nature is appointed as a mentor, and you would meet with that person every week or month to talk about your life and how you interpret this in the light of scripture and your on-going relationship with God. A director helps you place events and dynamics into perspective and can be a very encouraging spiritual presence in your life. Overseas, many religious workers cross denominational lines to obtain this kind of accompaniment. It is a very rich and sustaining relationship to find someone who can guide your spirit in a tumultuous time as this transition can be. Even if you have never had any spiritual direction in the past, or happen to be of a different denomination from someone you might like to accompany you, this would not be a problem to most men and women who guide others in this way.

Ties to home will continue to be very important for you while you are in Tupelo. News of your family and friends, how their lives are evolving, will be welcome the longer you are away Photos of your siblings' children, or your grandchildren can be doubly precious when distance holds you apart. But as time goes on it will be more and more difficult for you to write letters home. It will seem like peeling an onion. You need to explain so many layers before you get to the centre of what you want to communicate that it becomes easier to stick to superficialities—weather and news—than to talk about the ways your experience is affecting and transforming you. On the other hand, if someone visits from home, it can open the floodgate of letter-writing again for you after they've left. You can suddenly cut through the niceties and speak about your life as they've witnessed it.

If it doesn't seem like you are going to find the support you need from the people around you, or any other connection in your area that you have made, try to be faithful to letter-writing to one person back home, preferably one who is good about answering your letters. You will develop a very special relationship with this person, because you will share some of the most profound changes of your life with her or him, so choose that person with care.

A somewhat less reciprocal form of letter writing is to keep a journal for your self. It could be conversations with yourself, or a form of prayer, or just your thoughts of the day. It is important to be faithful to the writing, however, even if you don't feel like it, so that it becomes a part of the rhythm of your life. Some people find great resolution to their worries by putting their thoughts on paper. You can use a variety of questions to jump-start your writing on any particular day. Today I discovered. . .; Today I wish I had. . .; Today I'm thankful for. . . .

Both the journals and your letters will become a permanent record of your time in Tupelo and will be a tremendous comfort when you are back home and the longing is suddenly reversed. If you have stayed close to someone by letter, it would be very special to have that person visit you if at all possible. He or she already knows names and has your descriptions of characters and places, but a visit will cement that bond and it will become a source of future support as well. When you are back home and you miss your friends in Tupelo, this person more than any other will understand what you are going through. It may not ease the pain, but just being with them and talking about people, without having to explain elaborate bits of history as their eyes glaze over, will be enough.

Intimate relationships

While the impact of leaving family and friends behind and settling into a new place will be felt differently by each individual, it is certain that everyone will experience some period of profound loneliness in their new life overseas. Frequently, a single person might pursue an intimate relationship out of that loneliness, and the results are rarely positive. Consider declaring a complete moratorium on intimate relationships for the duration of your stay, especially if it is a short-term assignment. For longer-term placements, allow yourself to acclimate completely and to find your emotional stable ground again before contemplating starting an intimate relationship. Consult with your sending agency about its guidelines on this issue. Developing an intimate relationship with someone in your host country may be a rich and life-giving experience. It could also prove to be a distraction to your work and to your relationships within the broader community you have come to serve. Finally, consider how your behaviour in intimate and in all relationship reflects the faith that brought you to this place.

Lesbians and gays overseas

The reviews are mixed on this one: some people will claim that gays and lesbians almost have an easier time finding support in countries where homosexuality may be a less-than-familiar concept. A sub-culture can often find ways of connecting that are nearly invisible to outsiders. On the other hand, many cultures are intensely homophobic and people who have gone to great pains and personal cost to reveal themselves to friends and family back home may find themselves decades back in the closet in Tupelo. Gay and lesbian support groups can often be found in major cities in many parts of the world, but you may end up in a village where homosexuality is about as obscure as bungey jumping—more so, perhaps. As in North America, the presence of support groups or even a relatively visible gay and lesbian community does not necessarily mean wide acceptance in the society. Also, the church is often far behind progressive movements in the society advocating gay and lesbian rights and, indeed, is often virulently opposed to such movements. It is true, however, that gays and lesbians usually have come to accept a certain outsider feel in their lives; they may even have developed some superior coping skills that allow them to move back and forth with grace between belonging and not belonging, which is very valuable in a new culture. If you are gay or lesbian, you have lived with risk all of your life, so you will know when, or if ever, you will reveal yourself to someone in Tupelo. Be a bit more cautious than usual; you may come to enjoy the company of some very committed, justice-oriented and progressive men and women, whom you assume would have no difficulty with your homosexuality, but in fact the rights of gays and lesbians is nowhere on their agenda, and you may never get the chance to make the connection for them. Do remember, also, that some countries continue to outlaw homosexuality. The laws related to homosexual activity varies greatly from country to country and you should check out the situation before you go. Although you may not find it useful in other ways, the *Spartacus Guide* does give a reasonably up to date synopsis of the legal status of gay life in most countries as well as helpful information regarding support groups, health issues, etc.

One is the loneliest number

As important as new friends are for anyone moving into a new situation, you may find in your first six months that you are still quite alone. It takes time to connect with people at a deep and satisfying level, and unless you are very fortunate indeed to find someone who will become a long-term friend, you will need to rely on your inner resources to keep yourself content and balanced.

In this regard, there is no substitute for an intentional practice of prayer. Some need more time than others, and there are surely many ways to go about it, but a good rule of thumb is that it be daily and that it be given a priority, as much as food. You may be tempted to forget about the need to feed your spiritual hunger, particularly when so much about your new life is challenging and exhausting. Somehow, though, you need to make all of your struggles, questions and exhaustion part of your prayer, and give God the chance to speak amid everything else. There may be times, like Jesus at Gethsemane, when you are tempted to escape what confronts you. Your friends may seem far away and not interested. Yet God will see you through any challenge, and in trying to do God's will we take our part in fulfilling Jesus' own mission of love and compassion in the world.

Exercise

- What resources have you used in the past to get you through times of little support?

- What hobbies/activities could you pursue to get you circulating?

- Plan a time in the future when your closest friend or a family member will visit;

- Acknowledge small gestures of kindness;

- Plan to spend special days and events with someone, and explain that you don't want to be alone;

- Try to appreciate other ways of expressing faith or celebration, even though they may not be your style;

- Try to be observant in your prayer life.

to defend the cause
of the poor and needy

is this not what it means
to know God? Jer. 22

6 Vulnerable Times

*The thought of my affliction and my homelessness
is wormwood and gall!
My soul continually thinks of it
and is bowed down within me.
But this I call to mind,
and therefore I have hope:
The steadfast love of the Lord never ceases,
God's mercies never come to an end;
they are new every morning;
great is God's faithfulness.
"The Lord is my portion," says my soul,
"therefore I will hope in God."*

*The Lord is good to those who wait,
to the soul that seeks,
It is good that one should wait quietly
for the salvation of the Lord.*
Lamentations 3:19-26

You will be unusual indeed, if you sail through your time away without a wisp of misgiving, a week's subdued introspection, a full visitation of depression, or at the very least a nagging case of the blues now and then. There are bound to be events and situations that leave you vulnerable to self-doubt, frustration or even, in some cases, despair. Many people refer to this as "culture shock," which has a variety of stages, like those listed below and on the chart which follows.

Honeymoon: everything is fresh, exciting and energizing. You love the flowers; people are wonderfully welcoming and similarities stand out to you much more than differences.

Hostility: occurs anywhere from two weeks to six months into your experience and will be characterized by irritation with things different. You hate the fleas and ants; you can't make yourself understood; difficulties abound in every sphere. Some people will have trouble recognizing their own emotions at this time, but can observe physical signs of distress—feeling run down, susceptibility to illness, putting on weight, inability to sleep, irregular periods etc.

Adjustment: you are moving slowly from annoyance with the differences and difficulties presented to acceptance and gradual adaptation. This almost happens without notice—you begin to know your way around; the language is coming more easily and you are feeling more at peace within yourself.

Biculturalism: you are able to function in two cultures with confidence. The ways that bothered you a few months or a year back now have their own kind of logic and you enjoy and *almost* understand them.

U CURVE OF ADJUSTMENT

PRE DEPARTURE	ENTRY	3-6 MONTHS	7-18 MONTHS	PRE DEPARTURE
Normal Level of Emotional Equilibrium			Participators 40% Adjusters 50% Escapers 5% Serious Problems 5% Return	
Situation • planning • packing • processing • partying • parting	**Situation** "Explore" Stimulated tourist phase • meeting new people • seeing new places • hearing new sounds	**Situation** "Frustration" • novelty worn off • new people • strain • new places • new sounds	**Situation** Four Possible Outcomes: **Participators** Very effective, very involved, higher performance than normal	**Situation** Similar to pre-departure from Canada
Emotionally "Up & Down" • excited, enthused • but perhaps, fearful, sad at leaving • decreasing interest in present activities	**Emotionally** "Up" • excited • stimulated • fascinated • learning • experimenting	**Emotionally** "Down" • depressed • anxious • confused • angry • lonely • homesick • disenchanted • suspicious	**Adjustors** Self satisfied, do an adequate job but may reject environment **Escapers** Motivated by search for escape, reject home environment and seek to establish identity within a foreign environment	
Physically Weary but normal	**Physically** Perhaps some intestinal problems, insomia	**Physically** Develop colds, headaches, prone to take sick leave	**Serious Problems–Return** A few never learn to cope, develop emotional problems, often result in the need to return home	

Originally conceived by Clide Sargeant, with revision by Daniel Kealey.

It should be noted that the process of adjustment described here is common and to be expected among the vast majority of those crossing cultures. However, everyone's experience is unique; each person will pass through these stages at various rates, and with varying intensity. The time-line suggested here is arbitrary (based on the typical experience of someone going overseas for a period of about three years) so people going overseas for less time are likely to find the process somewhat contracted, though perhaps no less intense.

53

The danger of knowing these various stages of culture shock is akin to what students of medicine experience in their first year of study. Very often they develop an uncanny ability to identify the symptoms of the diseases they are studying in their own bodies. Suddenly they notice their glands are swollen, they feel weak, have night sweats and they're convinced they have a full-fledged case of the plague in downtown Burnaby In reality it likely isn't much more than a cold and sleep deprivation, but the knowledge can arouse an expectation that can jangle in the back of the mind.

Learning the stages of what has come to be known as culture shock may have a similar effect on you. You may not experience the symptoms in the ways that others have, or you may be looking for the honeymoon to end and the hostility to start and the power of suggestion provides all the symptoms you need. Ted Ward in *Living Overseas: A Book of Preparations* has some good insights into culture shock that are summarized in Appendix D.

Try to remember, whether you are experiencing culture shock or just a lonely time, that all of your life you've managed to cope with the slippage between the way you imagined it would be and the way it really is. Most people would call this the maturing process. Every shiny new pair of cowboy boots takes months to break in. And when the breaking-in is done, you're never quite sure if it was the boots or the feet that finally yielded. Every change, every increment of growth in our lives comes with some adjustment and pain. When it comes to your spirit, however, and when you're far from the comforts and support you know well, it's a little harder to be patient for the shift that will inevitably take you beyond a period of vulnerability.

Some people are water-bed worriers. Disappointment, fear or anxiety hits them at one edge of their lives and it rocks everything—a criticism of your work comes to you third-hand; it reminds you that no letters came this week, the water is off all day and you found another grey hair; why are you here anyway? Sometimes when worry sweeps into every corner of your being it takes a conscious effort to sit back and remind yourself about what sparked the spiral of self-doubt in the first place. When you've pin-pointed the spark, you can plan ways of dealing with it, or put it into perspective—file that away as experience.

Vulnerability can be exaggerated by illness, stress, unpredictability, loneliness and insecurity, all of which will be close friends of yours moving into a new culture and range of bacteria. In the rest of this chapter we will try to alert you to some reasons why you'll likely be confronted by a certain amount of vulnerability in your time overseas. You won't be able to avoid rough patches altogether, but you need to be responsible enough for your own well-being to do as much as possible to keep your perspective. That includes ensuring that you get enough rest, that you eat to stay healthy, that you balance work with pleasure, that you pursue hobbies and make time for friends and leisure. Beyond that, it's good to find a friend who can give you the assurance you need when it feels like your world is crumbling.

Future imperfect—language training

My mouth contorts
the word mashes through
plops out
and drops dead at my feet
mangled beyond recognition.
With hopeful eyes
I beseech my listeners.
Then, with the care of forensic linguists
they gingerly examine
my apparent attempt at communication
and solemnly offer their
astute guesses as to what
I might have been trying to say
                    Audrey Patterson

One of the first most challenging times that people encounter in overseas work is language school. In some cases you will be sent for language training to a third country or region that isn't anywhere near Tupelo. It's a lot like spending six weeks or six months in the waiting lounge of the airport, and your life can feel like it has been put on hold. In some cases, such as short-term people working in Asian countries where intensive language training over a full year would yield only a very basic vocabulary, you will not be given training at all and will be expected to manage with English or French alone. Worse still, you may end up in a place with no language training and no one who speaks English or French, so you must learn as much as possible with the point-and-bark method of language training. It's probably better to try to pick up a few books before you go, particularly if you know you won't be attending language school.

If you are obliged to learn a language that you have never studied before, it can be a humbling and humiliating experience, a drop-kick to your self esteem. For the first time, in years perhaps, you will be thrown back into the classroom to learn a new language—passive voice, gerunds, subjunctive, future imperfect—all of those aspects of language and literature that not many of us mastered in English or French. Even the mere thought of going back to school is daunting to some, with all of the inherent baggage of competition, memorization and examination, but in this case you've got a double handicap of not knowing the language you are being taught. Do you remember when you asked your Grade 5 teacher, Mr. Pittfield, how to spell misanthrope? He said, "Look it up in the dictionary." How do you look up a word you don't know how to spell? How do you learn a language without knowing the language?

No doubt there is a lot of memorization involved in the beginning, but even more than that, it's the student with a quick ability to make connections that is best suited to the task of language study. It isn't until you connect a phrase that you've heard in the classroom with something bandied across the supper table where you're lodged, or with something you read in your Bible, that you have really *learned* a phrase. In any case, you will find that language is very contextual; you will be able to have a conversation based on what you expect people to say and you'll probably manage just fine. "Hello, how are you, fine, how are you, fine, nice day, beautiful."

Rarely does it go, "Hello, how are you, fine, how are you, fine, I just saw a hippopotamus upstairs, nice day, beautiful." Even if someone did throw in that unexpected bit of news, you will find people for the most part exceedingly gracious with your efforts to know their language and will help you out wherever possible. Trust that.

A few rules will make language training more palatable:
- always learn greetings first and use them
- be willing to laugh at yourself
- be willing to have others laugh at you
- get some of the local children to help you with your numbers, colours and basic vocabulary
- be visible with your learning; people will be proud of you and help wherever possible.

One thing to be aware of about language school is that there is a profound longing for connectedness and for understanding there, and these very basic needs can cause any number of curious liaisons to emerge, particularly so for single people who are there without any support. The sheer anxiety of study and facing an unknown future can also raise hormonal levels excessively. You might begin to feel that you are shipwrecked on an island, and people are pairing off as if this were the last person they were going to meet for the rest of their lives. Remember that you may end up in language school with a variety of people from every profession with very different values. Some will have heard that the best way to learn a language is to become romantically involved with a language teacher or another local person. The theory does leave a lot to be desired about the *value* of people.

Don't misunderstand, some fine and lasting relationships have begun in language school because people meet each other on a level playing field with a lot of their normal barriers down. Many others, however, are the simple offering and receiving of a bit of comfort in a storm. You'll know the difference.

If you are a parent, your concentration may be divided between study, a one year old that puts everything in her mouth, a four year old who is clinging because he doesn't know anyone, and a ten year-old who is determined to return and live with her grandparents. There is a lot of adjusting to be made in this limbo of language school, and it's especially hard on people who feel some responsibility for the care and well-being of others. One constructive thing that can always be done is to offer comfort in listening. Acknowledge what each other is feeling. Be open with your spouse and children about your own fears and feelings. You may want to begin a ritual of time together after the evening meal, for example, where you sit on the porch and tell each other how the day has gone as you watch the sun set. These can be very precious times, and incredibly hilarious as you all put into perspective the many triumphs and pitfalls of a new language or a new culture. Prayer is another family ritual that can be very meaningful, where you celebrate each other, bring your cares before God who sees everything and knows us inside out. There you can name some of the fears of the little ones too, and they will feel heard.

As language training comes to a close you might find yourself packing again for a final destination. You may feel some normal resentment that you were just getting to know a group of people, in fact, feel remarkably close to them given the little bit of time you've spent together, marking some growth and achievement with them, and now you are faced with another round of goodbyes. Remember that transition and uprooting (even shallow roots) are hard on everyone. Don't expect to be always in control, to remember every detail. Try to be generous with yourself and what you must cope with.

It is very possible that mastering a few muttered phrases in a given language might not be the end of it for you: in Tupelo you may need to learn yet *another* language to communicate with the people you were sent to work with. This happens very often where a country was colonized by a European power. Most often the men know the language of the colonials, Portuguese or Spanish, but the women only speak an indigenous language and this becomes your next challenge when you are just about challenged-out. An indigenous language, having no resonance with English or French, will be the harder one to learn.

On the other hand, you may share a first language with the Tupelese, but among themselves they speak a *patois* that bears *almost* no relation to English or French. It's a two-way mirror and you're on the wrong side. They can almost understand you, but you cannot partake of their socializing and understand them. No one thinks you need language training because everyone speaks English or French there. Private lessons will probably be your best hope, and friends willing to slow their speech enough for you to catch the lilt.

Work in a new realm

There is no doubt that many North Americans get more self-definition from their work than almost any other aspect of their life. You've probably never gone to a meeting where you've been asked to state your name and something about the person who has most influenced your life; or attended a party where you were introduced as Pat Pizazz the worst watermelon seed spitter in Portage la Prairie. When it comes down to it we're a lot bigger than the work we do, but our occupation does determine our status. In Tupelo, where it might take you a year and a half to find your stride with a new language, understand why people do things the way they do them, and begin to function with limping competency, it's easy to lose confidence in this part of you that has provided such strong identity. In such cases the one step in front of the other approach is about the only formula for survival, with a reminder to celebrate patience and incremental accomplishments.

Family life in Tupelo

Coming to know and understand a different culture involves a number of things that you love immediately, some things that you miss instantly, and a handful of things that drive you to distraction. As you gain a more profound understanding of the people you have come to serve, you will find these three categories somewhat fluid: what bothered you at first has lost its edge; what you missed from home doesn't ache quite as much; what attracted you initially has another side. Record your observations in your journal; something from each of these categories each day, and watch to see how your yearnings shift over time—all but peanut butter, that is.

One of the things that will probably be in contrast to your own culture is the Tupelese's traditional family structure, where young adults live at home in an extended family until they marry. As a family you will be given the space you need for your own lifestyle. If you are a single person, however, or a couple without children, you may arouse curiosity, worry or protectiveness in those who live around you. The Tupelese will not be able to understand why you are living alone; in fact, the prospect of it might be terrifying to them. They will assume that you are very lonely, imaging themselves in the same situation, and will create a relay of people who will come to your house from sun-up to sun-down, when all you wanted to do was to hibernate with a good book.

Or someone might actually be assigned to spend time with you if there is any reason to fear for your safety This could seem like a major intrusion to people who are accustomed to being fairly private and calling their free time their own. You may need to check with your supervisor or colleagues to see if there is any reason why your living situation might be unsafe, and ask their counsel in managing the flow of visitors if it is not quite to your liking. Hospitality is a very important value in most cultures. Even closing your door during the day can be a very offensive gesture in some countries. So observe how others deal with guests and take your cues from them.

If you are single, and happily so, the other phenomenon in cultures where people always get married and marry early, is that there may be no satisfaction with your unmarried and/or childless state. (A couple without any children will often have the same status as a single person.) If the Tupelese themselves aren't trying to find you a partner, the expatriate community will have you matched and dispatched several times over. If you're happy with this kind of match-making you will do very well; if it irritates you, you'll need to try to make it clear, as inoffensively as possible, that you are happy as you are, or that you can do your own looking. Humour is often the best response in these situations.

Experience
People knew that I was single and it would come up among the women that they should find me a husband. All I needed to say to them was the old expression, "Better alone than a bad match." And all the women would say, "She's right, she's right" and never mention it again. -LR

Authority
Along with their family structure, it is very possible that the Tupelese will have a more traditional view of authority If you are a man, you may be invested with more authority than you need or want. If you are a woman, you may have less authority than you want or deserve. You may go out as an ordained minister in your own church, but because the church where you are going does not ordain women you are not able to function as a minister. Another form this might take is in decision-making. You may be accustomed to a great deal of consultation before decisions are made, but in Tupelo those decisions might be made by one person without any consultation whatsoever. And you may be the only person to whom it occurs to do things differently.

Experience
I was asked to preach at a neighbouring village. I had been really sick the night before, up all night. The women of the choir came to get me to go to the village which was about an hour away, singing and dancing as we went, with my pockets bulging with *Pepto-bismal*. We got to the village and the service was 45 minutes late starting. The service itself was three hours long and there was another hour's walk home. When it got to the point in the service where it was time for me to preach, I was introduced and I brought greetings from the church back home. Then the pastor said, "Now, in her country, which is the place where the sun sets, it's common and acceptable for women to be pastors and to preach. But that's very strange in our culture." And so he continued for the next 45 minutes to preach on his own. I never did get the opportunity to preach the sermon I had in my pocket. - MD

You may feel that you cannot compromise your values in situations where you are made to feel less than equal because of your gender. Your option then would probably be to consult with those who sent you and your colleagues in the area and explore other options for yourself. The response of some others who have been confronted with similar situations has been to seek other work in the area, teaching for example, where they have been able to contribute something at the local level, hoping that their influence and modeling might encourage another generation to see different possibilities for themselves. Others would see it as important to acknowledge the cultural differences but to stop short of any impulse to "change" the people you are going to work with or visit, until they themselves express the desire to do so.

Remind yourself that you are there primarily to learn and that you came into this venture with all the faith, good will and intention that you could muster. God is bigger than any situation, and despite what seem to be setbacks, it is inevitable that there are some valuable lessons for you to learn about yourself or your own denomination or culture from the overseas experience.

Conflict

Sometimes differences in values or working styles can escalate to the point where the work or your performance is compromised. It is always good to search out a confidante or a mentor who can help give you perspective on the situation. You may want to be very pragmatic about what changes are possible by confronting the situation; weigh very carefully what might be gained by what might be lost. You may find a person in authority is acting in inappropriate, illegal or immoral ways, but when you confront that person the result is that you and *your* work are suddenly roundly discredited, and all those who encouraged you to take on the issue have vanished into the woodwork. It's a lonely place.

Use your own good judgement from your past work situations. If conflict tends to immobilize you, it's probably a good idea to negotiate change in small ways. There is a great advantage to be gained by delaying confrontation until you have established trust and credibility within a situation, and that only comes with time. Maybe you will never influence those in authority, but you will encourage others around you who prefer your way of being and subscribe to your values.

In any situation of conflict it's good to remember the Jamaican saying, "behind the mountain there is another mountain." It should not dissuade us from taking on conflict situations, rather, it serves to remind us that in life conflict is permanent and inevitable, and when this dilemma is resolved, another will emerge.

Sexual cues in a new context

Sexual attraction and the cues to communicate this to another are the subject of countless psychology, sociology and literary texts within any culture. Add another cultural dimension and the complications are exponentially greater. Every kind of attraction and friendship involves the crossing of boundaries, the wooing across really—people allowing each other to see more of their real selves. This is both natural and one of the joys of finding a soul-mate at any stage of life. Across cultures, we need to be more sensitive to what is being communicated to us or what we are communicating. It is always a good idea to check out assumptions verbally, "when you said that, did you mean. . .?"

Different cultures have different expectations of personal space. It's important to get to know the norm in your new culture, to be able to judge whether or not you are being treated any differently than anyone else. It's also important to observe and ask what it means to touch or hug someone before doing so. It may be customary to greet each other with a bow, or a kiss, holding and shaking hands or exchanging breath. It may also be expected that two men or two women would walk hand in hand together, but not for a man and a woman to do so.

Experience
I was standing in the parking lot talking to the minister beside the largest church in town as people were streaming out of Sunday morning worship. Suddenly he grabbed my hand and as the conversation became more and more intense, his hand moved up my arm and our bodies came closer and closer. Although I thought I was a relatively open western male and aware of the difference in "personal space" needs in different cultures, my heart began to race and I began to sweat heavily and I looked for whatever excuse I could find to get away from him. This was just not how we did it at home. I have to admit, though, that by the time I returned I had adapted to walking hand in hand with other males and, very reluctantly, had to "unlearn" this behaviour and "keep my distance" again in public. -RF

Is this mutual?
The unfortunate part of attraction and crossing boundaries is that sometimes it is not mutual. Many organizations and churches have had to develop clear guidelines on sexual harassment, abuse and assault over the past few years. It reflects the sad rise in cases of abuse that are being reported.

Most church policy sets out zero-tolerance of relationships between clergy or church workers and those to whom they relate professionally. This would mean that you, as a representative of a church, are not in a position to enter into a relationship with someone in your congregation, if you are a pastor. If you are a teacher, you must not enter into a relationship with a student, even if he or she is an adult. In an office of another kind, you would not be at liberty to date a colleague.

Sexual harassment and abuse are seen largely as abuses of power, and foreigners are almost always in positions of power by virtue of their status as wealthy, educated visitors. It may feel mutual and consenting to you, but it could be seen by anyone from a distance as an abuse of your power. It isn't that relationships are suddenly forbidden, but safeguards must be put in place to protect people who might be vulnerable. In a growing number of North American churches, a minister is required to make public a developing personal relationship with a member of the congregation; the minister would then be moved to another church, or provision would be made for someone else to give pastoral care to the girlfriend/boyfriend elsewhere.

Victim of violence
There is another level of vulnerability that any of us faces in our own country as much as we do in Tupelo. At any time we could become the random victim of aggression, illness, a natural disaster, an accident or

a major political development. In the event of a natural disaster or political development (flood, earthquake, violent coup d'etat or attempted coup), you should follow these suggestions. These are only offered as a guide; you may need to modify them according to your situation:

- contact your supervisor/church to confirm your safety;
- have that person contact your sending organization back home;
- have that person also contact your family/friends back home, (even if it's a minor incident the news coverage may be sensational back home);
- check in with your embassy or consulate (in a pinch, any of the British, Canadian or United States embassies will do);
- if you are in danger, contact one of the embassies noted above for guidance and assistance;
- do not resist—comply with instructions of local authorities. Do not travel when instructed not to. Release any vehicle to local authorities if you are ordered to do so.
- you must comply with your supervisor if you are asked to leave the country. In the event that you must leave without prior consultation, your supervisor should be informed as soon as possible

Adapted from Canadian Crossroads International, 317 Adelaide Street West, Suite 500. Toronto, ON M5V 1P9. Toll Free: 1-877-967-1611. www.cciorg.ca. Used with permission.

Death

Relative to the numbers of people who travel and work overseas, foreigners are rarely the object of a terrorist attack. You are probably more at risk crossing a street in Tupelo's capital where safety standards for vehicles are substandard. There are some guidelines for procedures should an accident, an act of aggression or illness result in your death or the death of your spouse or your child. Prior to leaving North America, discuss who will take the necessary legal and moral responsibilities in the event of death. Make your wishes known to your spouse or a colleague so that someone knows who to contact and what to do for you. Put this information in a letter and leave it with someone to be opened in an emergency.

Personal violation

Personal violation, minor and major, is a more typical experience overseas. Petty theft by pick-pockets is very common where cities are crowded, where there is anonymity and overwhelming poverty. You might even have your home invaded by thieves who cart away everything including the clothes on the line and the gas tank from your stove. If you are confronted by someone who wants money or jewelry, always give it to them. Your life is worth so much more than heroics and material goods.

Experience

We came home one evening to find some of the kitchen ceiling scattered on the floor under a gaping hole where the roof tiles had been removed. The losses were upsetting, but the worst part of the experience of being robbed was knowing "our space" had been intruded upon. That day, I had finished using the tape recorder for language learning, and put it back in its shopping bag. Happily, they missed it. We had hollowed out an inconspicuous book for money and important documents; these were also missed by the thieves. But we learned the hard way not to leave jewelry in a box or scattered throughout the underwear drawer, and to always leave a light on, even when leaving the house during the day. -ME

As a woman you might be subject to an even further violation in the form of sexual harassment. Sexual harassment can manifest itself physically or psychologically. It can involve innuendo and gesture at one level, or unwanted touch or rape at another. There isn't any failsafe protection anywhere. Every woman knows that sexual harassment and rape happen everywhere. It doesn't matter if you are new to a country or if you've lived there all your life, if you dress modestly or not. You are as much at risk (perhaps more) of being harassed or raped by another foreign co-worker as with a total stranger from Tupelo. It is important to trust your instinct. Don't assume that you are missing cultural cues or being culturally insensitive if someone's physical gestures are making you uncomfortable. Also, it is helpful to have a confidante who can tell you what is acceptable or unacceptable behaviour, dress, language and discussion in your new context.

Despite all our best hopes for equality between the sexes, the burden still rests on the woman to act defensively and take every precaution for her self. A good defence is to observe very carefully the dress and behaviour of other women in the culture, possibly even take a Wendo self-defence course before you leave. Review your defences against sexual harassment in your own country. What strategies have worked for you in the past?

If you are the victim of sexual harassment, here are a few things you should do:

- Find a couple of supportive people to discuss the matter with;
- Ask their advice on how to confront the situation, (alone or with one of them?);
- Confront the person who is harassing you and verbalize your discomfort at the behaviour (if direct confrontation is inappropriate to the culture, find a third party who could act as an effective go-between);
- Ask that the behaviour stop;
- Keep track of dates and times, witnesses and other victims who might support you;
- Do not allow cultural sensitivity to excuse inappropriate behaviour.

If the situation persists and becomes intolerable for you, official intervention may be warranted; speak first with the mission or church authorities in the country, or you might need to seek the advice of a lawyer or approach the local police. Be sure to check the wisdom of this with your confidante (unfortunately, the police are not always a reliable source of care and protection, so never go alone). Finally, if there seems to be no other option, you should be in touch with your church or sending organization. They will want your safety put before all other considerations, and arrangements may be made for some counselling, to move you to some other location or for your return home if that is your wish. If the harassment results in rape, you must seek immediate medical attention and call a friend to be with you. Appendix F has some guidance in these matters.

People in other countries may have a skewed perception of North Americans that is fed by a diet of Hollywood movies, where most women and men become sexually involved within the first half-hour. They may think that all North Americans offer opportunities to test those perceptions. Use your own good common sense when you are offered special treatment by strangers. A payback is usually expected. Give unambiguous messages—don't smile when you are saying no. Rejection is handled differently in different cultures, but it is best to try to avoid finding yourself in a position to reject someone. Check with your confidant about situations that you are unsure of. What do you do if strangers invite themselves to your home? When do you need to impose the culture's own safeguards to a relationship that someone else might want but you do not. Check your assumptions with people by asking questions and insisting that they verbalize their intentions, "What does it mean to you when. . . ?" Also, it's important to remember that statistics show that most women are raped by men they know rather than total strangers.

As a man, you will be less often the target of overt sexual harassment than your women counterparts, still it does happen, and men should be prepared to find themselves in some very uncomfortable situations. You may be surprised to find that you are aggressively solicited to hire someone for sexual pleasures either on the street or in the privacy of your room. In Asia, it is not uncommon for men travelling alone to be awakened from a sound sleep by someone offering a long list of nighttime entertainments. In other places, people may feel very uncomfortable if you are a male and single; they may feel obliged to set you up with their cousin or even with a prostitute. It is often difficult to respond honestly and sensitively to these unusual situations. It is important that you are clear about your feelings on these matters but you also need to understand what is going on in the culture. Feel free to ask questions of someone you sense can appreciate your need to learn about the way things are done in your new setting. When asking someone out, remember that customs are different in every culture—asking someone out for a friendly evening at the movies may be construed to mean something more than you intended. Dating and courtship rituals vary from place to place, and so it makes ense to check out what your actions will mean in that particular setting. As a man, you are often in a privileged position, a position of power, and coming from the North you are often perceived as doubly so. Be careful not to abuse that position.

As a person, man or woman, it can feel very gratifying to be the object of another's affections and desires; it's hard not to be affected when someone seems very interested in and attentive to you. However, you may be perceived as a good mate for all the wrong reasons. You could be seen as a good catch because of your wealth, education or sheer exoticness. You could be a ticket out of a difficult situation. Remember that a good rule of thumb about intimate relationships overseas is: when in doubt, hesitate. It's better not to rush headlong into something with ramifications and dynamics at work that you can't understand, than to get involved in something that you may regret very deeply afterward. It is good to *'beware'* particularly in cross-cultural situations when you often can't *'be aware'*. Remember that you will feel alone and vulnerable in ways that you may never have in the past; and it will be much easier to surrender to your feelings without thinking things through clearly. If you err on the side of caution in these matters, you will likely be glad of it afterward.

Poverty
Finally, most overseas assignments will find you working in an area where there is a great gulf between the rich and the poor. And you, regardless of whether your income is a little or a lot, will be considered rich. You may be confronted daily with overwhelming need—and it's not for an extra pair of Nike air-pump sneakers, it's for something to go in that baby's stomach tonight. Everyone needs to find her or his own way of coping with seeing poverty all around them. Straight hand-outs can be problematic; it's not fair to set up dependencies particularly if you plan to pack up and leave some day. It's always good to pay for a service, insist on a service to make it reciprocal, even if it's for a street kid to watch your bicycle for five minutes as you go into the post office. There are some people who have neither rhyme nor reason to their giving. It all depends on how they feel that day. Others, on principle, give to their local parish or congregation and never to individuals on the street. Others still make conscious choices about how they will help: *always* when someone needs medicine or food; often concentrating on a few people they have come to know at some level.

Don't always expect that people are going to see you as a walking bank machine. Some will, but others will overwhelm you with their generosity, integrity and trustworthiness.

Experience
There was a constant lineup of people at my door. I tried to find some creative ways to distribute money which came to me from friends and church folk at home, and to encourage people to think of the money as a loan rather than as a gift. Still, the money going out was always more than the loan repayments and I felt

myself trapped in yet another form of dependency relationship. One day an old woman, the mother of one of my former students, called to me and tried to tell me something with little success. She made a gesture though, and I understood that it was about money. In frustration, I communicated to her to come to my office the following morning with her daughter who could speak my language and where we could talk about it. I was determined not to give any more because two years earlier I had loaned some money for a pig project and had not heard from them since. The following day, they arrived and just as I was about to say "No," in a very firm voice, the old woman pulled out a small bundle, untied the cloth around it and handed me my money, apologizing for being late and explaining that the pigs had died in the previous year's drought. **-RF**

In this chapter you have read about a lot of experiences of vulnerability, many of which you will have at least a brush with while you are overseas, but you will surely be able to add a few that we could never imagine. All such experiences can be dispiriting and unnerving. In combination, they can make you feel overwhelmed, ineffective and a failure at a personal level. Is there anything to be done? St. Thomas Aquinas who lived 800 years ago had some suggestions for days when all the food in the refrigerator has spoiled because the electricity is off again, someone spat at you in the market, a promising 13 year-old in your catechism class is pregnant, and the rains haven't stopped in a week. His cures for sadness include:

- any pleasure whatsoever
- the consolation of friends
- contemplation of truth
- tears
- a bath and a sleep

On a day like this you rummage in the bottom of your suitcase, take out that last Mars bar, put on a pot of Chinese tea, invite a friend over and listen to the best indie rock or classical, as the case may be. There are times when we need to do what we can to get through a patch. That's all. If it's more entrenched than that, you will need to do the same thing you would do back home, find some help or a professional to talk to.

In most cases you may just need to have faith that you will get through it. That's what faith is for: not the times where you know your way, when you feel comforted and connected to God. Now is the time to trust God, that you are working your heart out, with all your stars out. And you also need to trust that another Mars bar or something even better, will make its way to you before you will need it again.

Exercise

The following are some ideas to help you cope with feelings of culture shock:

- develop relationships on the basis of common need—food, housing, work activities, transportation;

- develop an understanding of the new culture, by talking to people, reading, visiting other parts of the country, etc.;

- respect difference; criticize in the privacy of your journal;

- find out what people value and learn more about it;

- acknowledge physical hardships; get suggestions from others as to how to manage them;

- plug away until feelings of strangeness diminish.

What are some of the things I could do to become more immersed in my new situation?

Who are some of the people I could enlist to help me?

Exercise adapted from *Canadian Crossroads International Participant's Handbook*, by Lynne E. Brennan. 1985, 317 Adelaide Street West, Suite 500. Toronto, ON M5V 1P9. Toll Free: 1-877-967-1611. www.cciorg.ca. Used with permission.

7 Transformation

There once was a gentle, holy man, a reformer. He studied the scriptures, lived and breathed them. When he came of age he became convinced that the religious men and women of his day, the leaders of his tribe, were adrift; they had lost their passion for God's way and their ability to read the holy books with wisdom. They had become legalistic instead, entangling their followers in the details of the holy laws—what was clean and unclean, what to do and not do on the Sabbath, who to associate with or not—rather than the spirit of those laws. The reformer read the books with perception, with an ability to separate wheat from chaff.

He gathered a small band of friends around him and walked countless dusty miles throughout his arid country talking to all who would listen to him about a new way to know God, a way of right relationship, a way of care for those in need. He helped many men and women see in different ways, ways that had meaning for them and set them on a new road. He fed those who hungered for truth and understanding. He opened the ears of those who were deaf, he healed people of their afflictions. He forgave when that was needed. And so it was most unusual, the day they arrived in Tyre, that he asked his friends to let no one know he was there. But neighbourhoods, being what they are, the word spread.

"He could not escape notice, but a woman whose little daughter had an unclean spirit immediately heard about him, and she came and bowed down at his feet. Now the woman was a gentile, of Syrophoenician origin. She begged him to cast the demon out of her daughter. He said to her, "Let the children be fed first, for it is not fair to take the children's food and throw it to the dogs." But she answered him, "Sir, even the dogs under the table eat the children's crumbs." Then he said to her, "For saying that, you may go—the demon has left your daughter." So she went home, found the child lying on the bed, and the demon gone." **Mark 7:24-30**

Jesus meets this woman for whom he feels no particular affinity. In fact, his language seems uncharacteristically harsh, using the metaphor of dogs to describe her place relative to the children of Israel. She is a foreigner, after all, and a woman. He has matters of consequence with his own tribe, enough to occupy him indefinitely. *This* is his calling. But the woman persists, and persists, and even though he is tired, and doesn't want to talk to anyone or be bothered that day, he does finally give her his attention. They sparr with words; he is challenged and moved by her faith. The passage is beautiful, unexpected, and the encounter leaves us wondering: could it be that this woman, this nobody, in some mysterious way has managed to influence Jesus, through her faith, to show him something more— unexpected—a new dimension to his mission, something larger than he originally imagined?

Ambiguity

Human nature tends toward a state of equilibrium. Like rebellious children bent on running away from home, we do not move too far away from what's predictable—about three village blocks—before we turn back to what is familiar even with its imperfections. If we enter a new situation or find ourselves in a sudden conflict, we employ all of our good skills of analysis to make sense of where we are and what is going on. We want to get back our equanimity, and understanding often helps us do that.

You are entering a world where all of those perceptive powers of analysis may not serve you as well as they do at home. You are entering a world where ambiguity will stand up and greet you at every street corner. You can wring those situations out, one by one, and hold them up for scrutiny against the values you have always held, and make judgments on them. But until you fully understand the values of Tupelo, or what motivates its people, your conclusions will have little foundation because they are based on your values. If you're the kind of person who has to have everything clear, settled or approved, you may find the overseas situation difficult. You will invariably come to conclusions that are very different from those of the Tupelese about things that are important to them.

The population question is a good example. Many groups from the West have concentrated on providing contraceptives and sex education to people in poor countries, in the belief that fewer babies to feed will leave more food for two or three healthier children. It has worked in the North; the standards of living and education have improved when the family's resources can be spread over fewer children.

If you talk to a mother of five in the mountains of Bolivia, however, you will learn a different perspective. Life is not so predictable there. She may manage from week to week or month to month on the edge of poverty, cultivating some vegetables, tending her sheep, but she is aware that any day her fortunes could change. She needs to raise children who will help her with the crops and animals, and she knows, as her neighbours know as anyone else in the village will tell you, you need to have six babies to raise two healthy ones to maturity. Life is like that. Does she take the gamble and have only two babies, feed them well, maybe send them to school to learn to read, then some unexpected illness or an abscessed tooth kill them as young adults when she is then too old to start over again? And who will take care of her if she ages as a childless woman?

Very often, we as outsiders think we have just the cure for all that ails the Tupelese. They just need a deeper well; they just need a vehicle to get them back and forth to the village; they just need. . . .There's nothing new in this, nor is there anything wrong with it particularly, if we can keep in perspective that countless "foreigners' great ideas" are sitting rusting throughout all the developing world and people pretty much go on living as they have in the past and as they will long after you have left. At the turn of the century, Albert Quirmbach, a missionary to China, decided that the problem of house fires in Leshan, a city in China's Sichuan province where he was posted, could be solved with a fire engine. Until then, with no running water in the city, a small grease fire in one kitchen could become a tragedy as it swept through the airy bamboo and wooden structures, leaping from house to house packed tightly along a city street.

The customary way of battling such blazes involved choosing a building several houses from the outbreak of the fire and feverishly tearing it down. Unable to leap the entire width of one home, the fire would burn itself out. Albert Quirmbach was an experienced missionary and had established cordial relations with the mayor of Leshan. After much persistence, Quirmbach convinced the city fathers of the merits of a fire engine.

Fund raising for a fire engine was just the kind of tangible good work that ignited benevolence in congregations back home. The fund-raising completed, Quirmbach ceremoniously presented the money to the Chinese. Somewhere, though, the all-too-common misunderstanding between the missionaries and the Chinese took place. It had nothing to do with Quirmbach's ability to understand the Chinese language; he was fluent. It had everything to do with the subtleties and nuances of a culture that are rarely comprehensible to the outsider. For the Chinese, the shortest distance between two points was not always a straight line. Between the city fathers' consent and the disbursement of funds, the Chinese decided that fire prevention was immeasurably better than fire fighting. With the church money, therefore, the mayor and city fathers solemnly erected a pagoda, to channel the wind and water influences, and prevent fires altogether. *

* Adapted from Katharine: A biography of Katharine Boehner Hockin, Wood Lake Books, © Heather Dau and Mary Rose Donnelly, 1991.

Cultivating humility

In the first two months of your time in Tupelo, you will have everything figured out: the political situation, the economy and where improvements can be made. In the next six months you will come to know some other factors that will confuse the political situation, complicate the economy and put a spanner in your strategies for improvement. If you are there three or six years, you'll be even less inclined to offer opinions about what you would do if you were managing things.

Humility isn't something we decide to put on like an extra pair of socks on a chilly night. It flows from empathy and is an attitude to be cultivated. We may be called on to reserve judgement and give others the benefit of the doubt that they have come to their conclusions and actions with integrity. Humility also comes from the knowledge that given the same background, resources and choices in any given situation that we would act in the same way as everybody else. That's hard to believe but true.

You may even discover, as the months pass, that the Tupelese, who labour so hard and struggle against such odds, have a great deal to teach you about actual living in the present. They celebrate one another, they take time, they look out for each other, they cry, they laugh, they die, they fall, they fail, are imprisoned and tortured, but they get up again and keep going. We're not sure we would, under similar circumstances.

Experience

The drive through Lima is like nothing I have ever seen before; pictures could not capture the squalor and the poverty. But to see the children and meet the smiles and the wonderful way that people greeted us shows that in the midst of poverty there is dignity and life. There is a foreign priest there, who has been in Lima for 13 years and is helping to organize a chain for peace, a human *cadena* that will hopefully span 20 kilometres of the highway through the barrios. Ironically, the radio program that will broadcast this event is also called *"Cadena."* The belief in solidarity - that a little cooperation can set off a chain reaction to link people together in the search for justice is wonderful. I am beginning to sense that the struggle to reach toward a dream of a better future and a new life are everywhere, and can be found with some searching in all spheres of society church, theology and education. Yet here they are more poignant and pressing. Here the need is so great, and the alternatives that exist if something new does not take shape are all very negative. The resilience of human beings continues to amaze me. . . .1 have felt the underlying conviction ever since I arrived in Lima that God wants to teach me something—to speak the word of truth that will lead me further along the way, the path to others, to God and to my deepest self.
-KA

Little by little you catch a glimpse of your own transformation in Tupelo. You discover how enriched you are by the voices and lives of the poor. Like the Syrophoenician woman, the challenge comes from the least likely place. Ironically, it's a call for *your* conversion. All your life you've been taught by your own culture that position and possession deserve your best years. You studied hard to become a professional; you bought a house, made all the responsible plans for your retirement, but they are all suddenly meaningless in this context. In Tupelo, where you entered their culture inarticulate and useless, you were welcomed for who you are, not for your efforts or accomplishments, not for the car you drive, nor the clothes you wear. All your life you've heard that you can do anything you want, if you just try hard enough. Here, you see lots of people trying harder than you could ever try, and they are still entangled in poverty. The systemic injustice is way beyond individual effort. There are too many factors against them. Yet, their spirits are unquenchable; they have faith and they are filled with hope. They celebrate one another, they take time, they look out for each other, cry, laugh, die, fall, fail and keep going.

Experience

When I went to Asia I believed that Christianity was about life and Buddhism was about death. Christianity gave hope for an after-life, whereas the only hope for life after death in Buddhism is based on ancestor worship. During my early years in Japan I found funerals, including Christian funerals, very difficult. The practice of people going up, one by one, to light a stick of incense and place it before the large photograph of the deceased on the altar, seemed pagan. Gradually I came to appreciate both the wake and the funeral. Death was discussed openly and the reminiscences brought the deceased person to life. I appreciated especially the fact that some churches, including my own, had "baptized" the Buddhist family altar found in most Japanese homes, by placing a cross on it. One special memory was the first anniversary of the death of a young father. The grandmother, the widow and two young children were present. We each were served a bowl of rice, whereupon the five year old boy said, "What about Daddy?" He took a bowl of rice and placed it on the small altar before his father's picture. There was a strong sense of a father who was with us but had gone a little ahead of us. **-MP**

The theologies of liberation that have been articulated in recent decades confirm your experience. They would say that the heart of the gospel is bringing good news to the poor - that you need to go out seeking justice with a preferential love of the poor in your heart, but also that your heart must be open to the transforming love of the poor. In fact, they would go much farther than your individual salvation. They would see that God's mission for the healing of all the nations will begin with the power of the Spirit already at work among the poor.

Experience

After many months of preparing, and after six months of language school in Bolivia, I remember that I went to my mission posting in Colombia feeling very inarticulate, somewhat fearful, and definitely not ready to handle the challenges that would come my way. And I was right. But nonetheless it was a tremendous time for me, a time of personal transformation. I was there only two weeks when my dearest friend, the man who had invited me to Colombia in the first place, the pastor of the church to which I had been assigned, was kidnapped. It was a nightmare living through those five days of his absence, not knowing if he had been killed or disappeared. What a relief when I answered the door almost a week later to find Francisco safely home; he was bearded and exhausted, but he was safe; it seemed a miracle. It was then, after it had come to my own house, that I realized what it truly felt to be a target of senseless violence, not knowing why, not understanding how it could be this way. I still don't. But that experience touched me very deeply. I was surprised to find myself two years later working for families of the

disappeared at a human rights office in Caracas. Many of my attitudes and beliefs were profoundly changed during the three years I lived and worked in Latin America. Somehow I want those changes to continue to shape my future in making decisions about how to live, where to work and how I treat others.
-KA

In many ways, the following passage from Jeremiah reminds us of what you have discovered in Tupelo, that all life is interconnected. Your salvation depends upon the salvation of others.

"Work for the good of the country to which I have exiled you; pray to Yahweh on its behalf, since on its welfare yours depends. For Yahweh says this: Only when the seventy years granted to Babylon are over, will I visit you and fulfill my promise in your favor by bringing you back to this place. I know the plans I have in mind for you—it is Yahweh who speaks—plans for peace, not disaster, reserving a future full of hope for you. Then when you call to me, and come to plead with me, I will listen to you. When you seek me you shall find me, when you seek me with all your heart; I will let you find me."
Jeremiah 29: 7-14

Exercise

- In what ways do you feel you have changed from your experience already?

- Where do you find resistance within yourself?

- Try to imagine how you might talk to your best friend about the things that bothered you so much four months ago, but seem less stressful now.

- Have a look back in your journal to a day six months ago, or two years ago. Read the passage and reflect on the changes you sense in yourself.

- Find a way to celebrate yourself—invite someone to a meal; go out for a meal.

- Write a long letter to someone you love back home and try to articulate four things you have discovered about yourself over this time in Tupelo.

8   In My End is My Beginning

Going home. You've given this moment a lot of thought over weeks, months, maybe even years. You were always expecting it to be a moment of distilled joy—back with family, back with those old friends you've missed so much, back to normal. After months or years of struggling with a new language, you say to yourself, "Oh, how nice it will be to be able to speak and be understood."

Sorry, there's some disappointment in the air: the band couldn't make it; the hall was double-booked; there's a shortage of ticker-tape, and, worse than all the rest combined, you still may not be understood when you open your mouth. This is a very unkind reality, but one that almost everyone experiences when they come back. If you thought you walked to the beat of a different drummer when you arrived in Tupelo, you're going to feel like a ballroom dancer in the Def Leopard Fan Club about this one. Most people expect culture shock when they go off; they're prepared for it. The part they almost never anticipate is that there is another culture shock that they will need to cope with on the other end of this experience, and the culture that shocks them is their own. If the stages of culture shock include a period of initial euphoria, followed by a long low, with ultimate coping, expect the long low to press in on you early upon your return. You won't get much sympathy for your re-entry turmoil, either; you're supposed to be grateful to be back.

How have things changed? People are always in a rush. They don't talk to each other; they never make time. They work outrageous hours to maintain a lifestyle of consumption; it seems to fill their void. Everything is disposable. Everyone uses voice mail and answering machines. You want to talk about your time away, but they couldn't in their wildest dreams imagine that you would miss that life. They say insensitive things, "You must be relieved to be back from there," or inane things, "you were so courageous to do that." Misunderstanding or subtle racism seems to creep into many conversations. You try to correct the perceptions and end up sounding cranky; people don't understand and so they avoid talking. They think you've changed. You have changed.

If there has been a death or a loss in your extended family while you were away, you will find yourself out of step with the grieving process. Everyone will have moved on in so many ways, but you will need to hear the stories, retrace the steps, say goodbye in your own way. It's as if you had been stuck in a time warp. Even if you haven't lost someone, you may very well feel out of step and in grief. .

Re-entry requires an equally intense adjustment, and so you it will be as important for you to find sources of support upon re-entry just as you did when you first went to Tupelo. If your denomination does not provide a formal re-entry program, you may want to look for counseling or group support focused on cultural readjustment for yourself.

Bring back your coping skills

Begin with those who sent you off in the first place, a church or secular organization struggling for justice in some area of your country or globally. Try to connect with someone in your town or city who has had a similar overseas experience. They will hear you in a different way from most, because they've likely been through this themselves. Find that person you wrote to most faithfully, or who visited you in Tupelo, and talk his or her ear off.

Experience

Friends, a family of six, came to visit us in Asia on their way back home after two years in the Middle East with a secular company. While overseas they had been deeply involved in the local "underground" church. They stayed with us for ten days and we heard about all their experiences. Before they left we cautioned them that they might not have as attentive an audience when they returned home. One Sunday afternoon, a few months later, we received a long-distance telephone call from them. No one, family or friends, seemed interested in their stories after the first five or ten minutes, and they needed to reconnect with people who recognized the significance and uniqueness of their experience overseas. -ME

The next step is to get involved in some work or some volunteer capacity that will allow you to use this gift of global awareness that you have cultivated over a few months or years overseas. If you've ever played the role of mediator in your family, explaining this brother's meaning to that sister's offence, then you will find yourself beginning to do that on a cultural level, becoming a mediator of difference. You will be surprised around the supper table, or at coffee break in the office, or at a meeting of parents and teachers, that people reveal a great deal of lurking racism in their remarks—the part about them taking jobs from *us*, or *them* fighting their battles over here. You will find yourself, sometimes patiently, explaining the other side of the situation to your family, to your friends, to co-workers. All over again you will find yourself not quite fitting in. The jokes aren't funny; the convenience food you find unpalatable; you want to live simply and everyone wants you to get a car.

If you live in an urban centre, chances are good that you will hear Chinese, Spanish, Portuguese, maybe even Swahili from time to time on local buses or the subway. If you are in a more rural location, you may need to find a way of connecting with a group from Tupelo in your region. Call the closest embassy, or check through denominational contacts. You may even be able to subscribe to periodicals from regions that will keep you in touch with the news more than is reported by the major media.

Staying connected to this experience is vital, otherwise, a year later you may wonder what happened to that part of your life. You will even sense some guilt if you immerse yourself into this culture about which you had grown to have misgivings. You owe it to yourself to maintain some fidelity to the things you have learned and the people you have loved in Tupelo. At this stage of your journey there is a companion book to this one that will help you work through the process of return, with all its disappointment, anger and grief. It's called *Coming Home*, and you'll find details about it in the bibliography. If you've been away for a shorter term, there is a video that might work just as well; details about *"Making Contact"* are also found in the bibliography. These will help you synthesize the past few months or years a bit; help you stay in touch with the experience and what you have learned from it.

There is no doubt that feeling outside may be forever part of your life. It is known as being from a "third culture" – neither from here nor from there. You have come back to your culture as an outsider, with a very different perspective on your old way of life. It may be hard to imagine, but this otherness in your way of being and seeing is a gift to your society. You have known a lifestyle or learned some values that will enrich your family and work life. You have coping skills way beyond most people you know. You have a profound awareness of the interconnectedness of all parts of the world, and you will work for understanding and justice among all those you meet and touch. And finally, you will make connections to all parts of your life—the food you buy, the language you speak, the justice issues you pursue in your own country. You may not see yourself getting back to Tupelo in the near future, but your friends there will know with confidence that they have an advocate and friend working for global justice where it matters.

Exercise

What good coping skills have you learned over the years to help you through this time?

What rituals or routines did you establish for yourself or your family to help articulate what you and they were feeling during the transition?

Name three people that you will make a special effort to connect with back home.

How will you help your partner and children through this transition?

What is the Spirit calling you to or beyond at this moment in your life?

9   Appendices

Appendix A

A Cursory Look at Mission History in the 20ᵗʰ and 21ˢᵗ Centuries

The challenges and opportunities experienced by contemporary mission personnel are products of centuries of mission history. Mission over hundreds of years has shaped and continues to shape both the sending and receiving churches and cultures. In order to work respectfully and effectively in mission, it is essential to understand this rich and complex history of global mission as well as the particular nuances of mission history experienced by any given culture, country, or church. As a starting point, a brief overview of the past century might look like this:

As individuals set out in mission at the beginning of the twentieth century, they likely went out with the expectation of evangelizing the world within their generation, believing that they were taking Christ to heathen people. The great commission of Matthew 28:19 would have been their inspiration and assurance, *"Go therefore and make disciples of all, baptising them in the name of the Father and of the Son and of the Holy Spirit, teaching them to observe all that I have commanded you, and lo, I am with you always to the close of the age."* Converting *them* meant teaching them that they were sinners, (as sin was a foreign concept in some cultures) and then teaching them how to renounce their sinful ways. Unfortunately, the earliest missionaries often had to make their way to these lands on the boats of traders and mercenaries. They may have chosen otherwise if there had been other options for transportation, but there were none. It was hard, therefore, for local people not to assume collusion, to separate out the more trustworthy from the less-than-trustworthy.

Within a decade, missionaries were referring more frequently to John 3:16 as their motivation instead of the great commission, *"God so loved the world that God gave God's only son, that whosoever believes in him should not perish but have eternal life."* It was somehow more positive to enable souls to live eternally than teach people what they shouldn't do. That generation of missionary would likely have been a teacher as an evangelist. After 20 years in some mission fields, you could count the numbers of converts on the hands of all the mission personnel. Evangelism continued, but education was on the rise as the new way to reach people. In order to gain entrance into the foreign schools, however, the Chinese, Africans and Native Americans often had to relinquish their own beliefs and the traditions that the foreigners found offensive. As in the case of Indigenous people, we've come to understand this as cultural aggression. In addition it has taken many years to recognize that it was impossible not to impart European or Western values and beliefs at the same time.

Somewhere in the decades between the two world wars, the liberal denominations began to emphasize the churches' contribution to world peace over personal salvation. They saw themselves as reconcilers and took II Corinthians 5:19 as their standard: *"God was in Christ reconciling the world to God, not counting their trespasses against them, and entrusting to us the ministry of reconciliation."* Missionary personnel going forth after World War II probably were medical doctors or community development workers with particular skills to address deficiencies and to improve the health and living conditions of the mission hosts.

The West had lost a great deal of moral ground during the Second World War as the atrocities and deeds of Christian countries were revealed to the world. Many missionaries turned their efforts to reconstruction and to the social well-being of those they went to serve. They thought that by modelling service they would be known by their love. Hospitals were built, agricultural projects begun and the array of elementary and secondary education was broadened to offer post-secondary education in the hope that the missionaries' brand of service and sacrifice might be communicated to a new class of local professionals. These overseas workers were impelled by personal witness— not speaking so overtly about conversion and Jesus as Lord, but motivated by a personal allegiance to Christ—they were committed to the work and well-being of the people they had come to serve and motivated by private Gospel values. Nevertheless, even though they might have saved countless babies by encouraging their mothers to breast feed instead of giving them tea and sugar, the missionaries would still be open to criticism that they were promoting Western technology, values and ideology.

The 1950s and 60s brought a profound change to the world church. The post-war wave of technical assistance evolved into something with a wider world church flavour. The World Council of Churches had been formed which would move churches toward the notion that peace is not possible without justice in the world. This was mirrored in the Roman Catholic Church's Second Vatican Council that saw the Catholic church opened and encouraged to take on a role that was quite a bit more grounded in the needs of the world. Matthew 25:35 became a motivator for many Christians, *"for I was hungry and you gave me food; I was thirsty and you gave me to drink; I was a stranger and you welcomed me, when naked you clothed me; when I was ill you came to my help, when in prison you visited me."* It wasn't enough to seek personal salvation; dignity in food, shelter and clothing were also a minimum for everyone. Ironically, this concept of a wider church was coming about as the political world was dividing along East and West lines. The result was that many peoples suffered atrocities under governments being wooed, and heavily armed, by one or other of the major powers.

By the late 60s and early 70s, national churches were claiming their own life and authority. The interconnectedness of the world became clearer as Christians and others of good will in the West began to analyze the various systems that created hardship and poverty for people in other countries. Churches in other countries were asking for a new kind of accompaniment; they were asking their friends in the West to stand with them in solidarity. It was a concept that would be made concrete in efforts by the churches to influence their own government policies that provided arms or supported with loans governments that denied the human rights of their people in order to stay in power. Jesus' words in the Synagogue at Nazareth, echoing Isaiah, provided the stance for a more prophetic form of Christianity, *"The Spirit of the Lord is upon me, because it has anointed me to preach good news to the poor, it has sent me to proclaim release to the captives and recovering of sight to the blind, to set at liberty those who are oppressed to proclaim the acceptable year of the Lord."*

At the end of the 20th Century, the notions of accompaniment and solidarity were amplified. There was a growing realization throughout the world that we need one another to solve the global problems that we face. A destroyed ozone layer will affect every region, regardless of national boundaries. This and other global problems are too large for any one country to resolve, or any affluent country to guard itself against. On the level of denominations, there was a greater effort to engage friends in other countries in discussions of new mission directions. This emerging mutuality in our mission led to new expressions of mission within denominations. Some began to invite missionaries from other countries to help us see ourselves through new eyes. There was a growing sense that North and South, East and West must work together to build global partnerships if churches are to respond prophetically to the gospel imperative of the Beatitudes in Matthew 5:3, *"How happy are the poor in Spirit, theirs is the kingdom of heaven"* which invites us all to experience our brokenness and need for one another.

The beginning of the 21st Century is both an exciting and confounding moment in mission history. It is not possible to name one approach to mission and, in fact, it is not difficult to find many of the historical approaches being used and shaped anew along side emerging new approaches. One is reminded of the Pentecost story in Acts 2, *"All of them were filled with the Holy Spirit and began to speak in other languages as the Spirit gave them ability."* There often is little consensus and some confusion, so much so that it may appear that we are not all working on the same project, that we, in fact, may be working at odds with one another. At first glance, their may be a temptation to react in a way similar to the crowd in the Pentecost story. When they saw the confusion of languages being spoken, they *"sneered and said they are full of new wine".* There is also great hope and excitement in today's moment in Mission History. Although there are many different approaches or "languages' of mission we can trust the Holy Spirit is at work.

Today one dynamic is the emergence of new "theologies" in countries that were once the subjects of mission activity. In these theologies one may see the influence of previous missionaries, but also other influences including approaches to the Christian faith shaped by the context and culture of these countries. In many cases there is tension and disagreement between the churches that used to be the senders and the receivers of missionaries.

Mission activity today is impacted by the changing role and the questioning of the role of the churches in cultures that historically sent missionaries. While churches in these countries may be seeing a decrease in their power and influence, many of the churches that were receivers of missionaries now hold a central role in their culture. While church membership and activity is on the decline in many countries, it is often experiencing impressive growth in countries that were once the objects of mission activity.

Twenty-first century mission is shaped by an unprecedented access to travel by some of the world. In the past there were relatively small numbers of missionaries, usually under the direct umbrella of denominations or missionary societies. Today there is an explosion of mission activity such as mission trips, work trips, study tours, relationships between congregations, and Mission organizations which operate outside the denominations. A large number of Christians also travel the world for work or as tourists.

Mission has been influenced by a changing global reality. Technology such as the internet and changing news media has brought previously unthinkable access to the world. Culture, including Christianity, can change and shape other cultures through these technologies and media. The global economy is such that the actions, lifestyles, and purchases of one group of people can have a significant immediate impact on other peoples. There are movements of people on a global scale that have led to many cultures and faiths living side by side in places that were once relatively homogenous. For many who live in countries that once were the primary senders of missionaries, they find they have people in their city or neighbourhood from countries that would have once been the receivers of those missionaries.

From this confusion there may or may not emerge a consensus or pattern of mission activity in the twenty-first century as some approaches fade and others thrive. Just as those present during the Pentecost story would not have been able to imagine what lay ahead for Christianity, so also we may be surprised by what lies ahead. Twenty-first century mission activity is shaped by many people responding faithfully and in many different ways to today's world. Mission is done trusting that God is active and present in this confusion just as God was present through the Holy Spirit in the Pentecost story.

Appendix B

Christianity's mission in the world today faces a crisis. In every age such crises have arisen and new movements have emerged within the church, under the guidance of the Holy Spirit, calling people to follow Jesus Christ in witnessing to God's love for humankind. In the early church, when Christians became too closely identified with the doubtful blessings offered by the Roman state, the monastic movement reminded them of Jesus' world-denying thirst for righteousness and the coming of God's rule on earth. Such reform movements have recurred regularly throughout history, reminding Christians that God's mission is never completed. The leaders of the Protestant Reformation reflected this belief when they adopted the slogan *Ecclesia semper reformanda* (The church must always be reformed). And Jesus emphasized this open-ended view of the Christian mission when he taught us to pray constantly, "May your rule be established (Thy kingdom come); your will be done on earth as it is in heaven."

One aspect of the contemporary crisis is the perception that the great missionary movement, which began in our modern Western world, to make the Good News of God's love in Jesus Christ known throughout the earth, appears to have run down. With the possible exception of some conservative evangelicals, fewer and fewer people are offering themselves for overseas service. In Japan, the decline began as early as 1956. By 1985 the trend had become worldwide. Offerings for missions declined, although they were somewhat balanced by increased contributions to other humanitarian enterprises.

Surveys, such as the study by Reginald Bibby entitled *Fragmented Gods,* suggest that Canadians see the church primarily as an organization placed in the local community to serve their needs, rather than as the body of those who have been called to follow Christ by living a changed life. As with the supermarket, they want the local parish to be there whenever they want to call on it: to baptize their children and marry them when they grow up; to counsel them in trouble and bury them when they die. A few will attend a Sunday service (especially on the great feasts such as Christmas or Easter), but they see that as a time of quiet or celebration, when they can escape from the everyday world of competition, strife, and change. So, naturally, they do not welcome sermons which disturb that quiet by raising issues related to the outside world such as the Christian's mission, or the abolition of poverty and injustice.

Even the minority of people who go to church regularly and take their faith seriously find it difficult to make up their minds exactly how the church's mission is to be conducted. For some, the old ideas no longer seem to work. The ties in the past of overseas missions with imperialism make them feel guilty, while a closer contact with non-Christian religions makes a mission aimed simplistically at proselytizing problematic. Yet neither are they satisfied to substitute for it a program of vague humanitarianism which seems always in danger of spilling over into paternalism. Many of us gaze with envy at what seems like the simple faith of the conservative evangelicals who still follow what they firmly believe to be *The Gospel* with its Great Commission to go and make disciples of all nations, baptizing them in the name of the Father, and of the Son, and of the Holy Ghost. Have we somehow fallen away from the faith of our ancestors?

Before we can answer that question, however, we must review in some detail what has come to be called the "traditional" view of mission. (I have put the term in quotation marks because this is actually a view which gained full acceptance among non-Roman Catholics less than two hundred years ago—a short period in the two-thousand-year-old history of Christianity—when the English Baptist, William Carey, wrote his stirring tact, *An Enquiry into the Obligation of Christians to Use Means for the Conversion of the Heathen.*) To summarize this view, the modern missionary movement which carried out the great expansion of Christianity from post-medieval Europe and America operated on the basis of four broad assumptions:

1. It was responding to the command of Jesus (the Great Commission), "Go ye into all the world and preach the gospel to every creature" (Mark 16:15; also Matthew 28:19 and Luke 24:47).

2. It was the duty of all Christians to obey that command, but it could be fulfilled in different ways. By a convenient kind of division of labour, overseas service was seen as the special vocation of an elite group, the missionaries, while ordinary Christians could obey by supporting overseas work with money and prayer.

3. The world was divided into two large geographical areas: Christendom, whose belief and culture were Christian, and Heathendom, whose inhabitants lived in constant danger of eternal damnation if they did not have the gospel preached to them. In the tradition of the medieval Crusades, mission was seen as territorial expansion through the conquest of Heathendom. Usually such expansion was seen in terms of the organized outreach of an institutional church which was transplanted, with all its (Western) cultural accoutrements, onto the new soil.

4. Expansion took place by means of the conversion of individuals. Conversion was seen primarily as a person's rejection of the old idols and the acceptance of Jesus Christ as Lord and Saviour, the One who atoned for their sins by his death. The new life was expressed in otherworldly terms as the plucking of an individual soul out of a sinful world (the old, "heathen" culture) and preparing him/her for heaven by introduction into the "Christian" life of the church.

The above assumptions were held within a context of a highly complex pattern of economic, political, and ideological forces which were continually shifting their relation to one another as societies developed. At the risk of oversimplification, however, it can be said that almost all missionary enterprises in the Western world since the end of the Middle Ages began within the context of some prior commercial or colonial commitment on the part of the nations in which they arose. The celebration of the five-hundredth anniversary of Columbus' arrival in the Americas has shown how inextricably intertwined were the motives of missionaries and explorers. As one conquistador, Bernal Diaz, expressed it, Europeans went to the New World "to serve God and His Majesty, to give light to those who were in darkness, and to grow rich, as all men desire to do." For many, whether among the colonizers or the colonized, the spread of Christianity and that of Western civilization appeared to be indistinguishable. As the famous missionary David Livingstone announced to the students at Cambridge University in 1858, "I go back to Africa to make an open path for commerce and Christianity."

The inability to distinguish between the two movements led to other attitudes, such as racial superiority. The Industrial Revolution in the West gave increasing technological power to the colonizing nations. Missionaries were courted by the peoples to whom they went because of the tools and machines they possessed and the literacy needed to operate them. As Stephen Neill pointed out, in 1818 the King of Madagascar was more interested in the ability of David Jones of the London Missionary Society to bring in bricklayers, ironworkers, and a printing press than he was in the Christianity they professed. When Christianity seemed to be attracting attention, the regime began a violent persecution and all evangelism in the country was halted for a generation.

All missionaries, whether they wanted it or not, had behind them the armed might of the industrialized nations. In China, for instance, permission for missionaries to proceed into the interior to carry on their work was written into a series of "unequal treaties" which were forced on the country following its defeat in wars between 1842 and 1900. The rising standard of living in the West which resulted from a combination of technology and capitalist financial accumulation came to be interpreted by all Europeans—including missionaries—as "civilization." This quality, somehow associated with the spiritual blessings of the gospel, made them feel superior to the "heathen" cultures they encountered.

How this superiority manifested itself in missionary practice began to become evident toward the end of the nineteenth century. For example, when the first African bishop, Samuel Adjai Crowther, died in 1891, the missionaries in the field opposed the election of another African. An earlier generation had seen nothing but gain in the choice of an indigenous leader as distinguished as Crowther. But a younger generation, accustomed to the "blessings" of what we would today call a more developed society, argued that no African was as yet equal in Christian nurture to a European. . . .

Today the commercial and colonial empires are breaking up following half a century of political and economic upheaval which has led to two world wars and innumerable local conflicts. The struggles for freedom and independence on the part of those nations once dominated by the West have placed the church in what we now call the Third World in a position that is, to say the least, ambiguous, and have called our accepted assumptions about mission into question. The contradiction between the liberating message of the gospel and the actual position of indigenous Christians, as members of churches which represent institutional extensions of Western society, has placed many in a situation of conflict that has become almost intolerable for them. Many places have responded by founding independent, sectarian churches. In the case of one nation, China, this clash has resulted in the total disappearance of the traditional denominational structure of Protestantism, and a situation close to schism for Roman Catholics. Even in those countries where some institutional connection remains, leaders who were once obedient servants of a Western-style enterprise now deny customs or structures which appear to them to be relics of colonial days. And the contradictions are not allayed by the continued bondage to the great international, commercial conglomerates in which third-world societies find themselves.

The contradictions between preaching and practice become painfully clear when we survey the world as it exists after five hundred years of Western, Christian missionary activity. Where we preached salvation (liberation), we have brought colonial and economic oppression. Even though a measure of political autonomy may have been achieved by many of the states of Africa and Asia, the gap in standard of living between those nations and the affluent countries of Europe and America continues to grow. Where we preached peace, a crescendo of warfare has ensued. The conflicts raging in Angola, Somalia, and the Soudan; the continued activity of right-wing death squads in Central America (and many other places) can all be related to the aftermath of the colonial era.

We have extolled the blessedness of the poor while we increasingly profited and grew rich at their expense. Trade practices which turned third-world countries like the Philippines or Brazil into supply areas for the affluent North; fiscal policies in our own country which have increased unemployment: all these have led to a growing gap between rich and poor. Where we promised that in Christ there would be no difference of race or class, we have raised up whole states such as South Africa, or situations such as those in which our own Indigenous people find themselves, founded on racial discrimination and domination of the many by the privileged few. As Christians we stood by and washed our hands of the excesses of imperialism, but we did not reject the riches which accrued as a result. As Helmut Gollwitzer has pointed out, it is that part of the world which we have called heathen that stands today in the place of the poor man, Lazarus, whom God took to Abraham's bosom, which the Christian nations look like the rich man whom Jesus said God condemned to everlasting fire (Luke 16:23).

In this context, a chorus of voices from the Third World is forcing us as Christians to rethink the assumptions about mission that we have been calling traditional. The truth of each one of the basic principles we have summarized has been questioned and found wanting.

1. Our emphasis on the Great Commission as an imperative for mission has allowed us to stress what we do to others, making the communication of the gospel seem like a one-way process. *We* became the bearers of truth to the ignorant heathen. A young Baptist pastor from West Africa described how his people were taught to despise their own way of life. "The missionaries behaved," he said, "as if only they knew God's will. Throughout our centuries of history it was as if God had completely neglected us."

Yet many other aspects of Christ's teaching reveal a quite different, more reciprocal, or two-way approach. When people came to Jesus for help, his first words to them were often in the form of a question, "What do you think?" (e.g., Mark 9:21,10:3; Luke 10:26). Jesus used parables to announce the kingdom because their interpretation required participation and response from the hearer (Matthew 13:34).

St. Paul describes Jesus' mission in terms far more compatible with the obscurity it actually endured than the triumphalist assumptions that have characterized so much modern missionary thinking (historical records of the time hardly mention Jesus, allowing some modern critics to doubt whether he actually existed at all). "God sent his Son, born of a woman, born under the law" (Galatians 4:4). "[Jesus Christ]. . .made himself nothing, assuming the nature of a slave" (Philippians 2:7). In contrast to the mighty technological and economic power that has stood behind the modern missionary movement, Jesus constantly identified himself with the powerless "little ones": children (Mark 9:33-37, 10:13-16); women (Mark 14:3-9; Luke 7:36-50; Mark 15:40-41, 16:1-8; Luke 8:1-3); the poor (Luke 6:20,16:19-31), and social outcasts (Mark 2:15-17; Matthew 21:32).

Incidentally, did the Great Commission actually represent Jesus' primary command to his disciples? If it did, why then did those same disciples have such a hard time making up their minds whether or not it would be right to take the gospel to the Gentiles (Acts 11:1-4, 15:1-29; Galatians 2:1-10)? Modern New Testament scholars draw a clear distinction between pre-and post-resurrection sayings of Jesus. In the case of the latter, Christ's actual words and the early church's interpretation have become closely identified. It is not at all clear that the historical Jesus approved of taking the gospel outside the Jewish nation. What about his reply to the Syrophoenician woman (Mark 7:27)? Or Matthew 23:15, "You travel over sea and land to make a single convert [literally, a proselyte]; and you make the new convert twice as much a child of hell as yourselves"? Yet once the leap from Judaism to the Gentiles was made by Peter, Paul, and the others, it became clear that the church was acting in Christ's Spirit (Acts 11:1-18).

2. Over against the "special vocation" assumption, the theology of the New Testament makes clear that all who have been made members of Christ in baptism become participants in the divine mission (John 10:21-22; IPeter 2:9). As we bear Christ's cross we follow Jesus, "to

bring good news to the poor. . . to proclaim release to the captives and recovery of sight to the blind, to let the oppressed go free, [and] to proclaim the year of Jubilee" (Luke 4:18-19).

These words place Jesus in the tradition of the prophets of the Hebrew Scriptures (in the above passage Jesus is quoting from Isaiah 61) who proclaimed God's judgment on the economic and political structures of their day. The reference of the Year of Jubilee comes from Leviticus 25. There all practising Jews were commanded every forty-nine years to pronounce—among other things—a moratorium on debts, in which all slaves would be freed and land lost through debt would be returned to its original owner. In other words, the gap between rich and poor would be abolished. Of course, historically, the facts of life made this command a kind of dream. But Jesus is here saying that in the commonwealth of God which he is bringing, this dream will come true.

So to follow Christ will certainly involve all Christians in personal witness and the conversion of individuals. But such witness will also include involvement in the struggles for economic justice and political liberation that are going on today all around us; struggles against racism and poverty and sexism in our own country as well as solidarity with similar movements in Asia, Africa, and Latin America.

3. Modern insight into the evils of imperialism and the human suffering attendant on the industrial development of the West now make it impossible to accept the former, clear division of the world into Christian and Heathen. . . It is a contradiction in terms to call one part of the world Christian and another Heathen. Certainly, all Christians are sent on God's mission. But God is also already present in every part of the world and has been active in creating every culture (John 1:3). Thus, the Christian from the West who goes to another country needs always to be sensitive to what God has already done there, and not try to foist his or her own customs on it, just because they are familiar. Not only are we in the West meant to "help people out there" but we are also to proclaim God's judgment on injustice in our own economic and political institutions which we now see to be oppressing the very people we have been sent to aid.

Nor can we look upon one culture as being more Christian than another, as did our missionary forebears when they dressed the people of Africa or the Pacific Islands in European clothes. That kind of assumption lay behind the practice of making proselytes which both Jesus and Paul rejected (Matthew 23:15; Galatians 3:28). All humanity has been made in God's image (Genesis 1:27). The Spirit blows where it will (John 3:8) and works to redeem all cultures. Cultural imperialism is no better than political or economic imperialism.

4. Accordingly, conversion means the "turning" to God of a person, through the grace of Christ, *within the totality of his/her own culture* (Romans 12:1-2); a change in life which includes external behaviour as well as internal transformation. Conversion is the opposite of proselytism, which seeks to take persons *out* of their own culture and implant them into ours. Conversion is the beginning of a process of growth through which God works to redeem all people *within* the culture in which they live, with all the distinctive customs and practices which those cultures have developed through history. Because Christianity in the Third World is beginning to show us what this means today, we are witnessing an exciting, new phenomenon of plurality and abundance of gifts, such as has never existed before in history.

Yet precisely because this phenomenon is so new, it may become a problem for us in the West. The dismay displayed by many Western delegates to the 1991 Canberra Assembly of the World Council of Churches at the apparent "syncretism" of a theological presentation by the Korean, woman theologian Chung Hyun Kyung illustrates this problem. For centuries we have been accustomed to understand our form of Christianity as absolute and normative. So it shocks us to find others developing a different interpretation (e.g., of the person of Christ) or worshipping in different ways (dancing during a service in Africa or Korea; letting off firecrackers at the eucharist in the Philippines!). But, as the Chinese theologian C.S. Song has written, if we believe in a Christ through whom *all* things were made (John 1:3), we can no longer say that only the Western form is normative.

Consequently, articles of belief such as creeds, once seen as basic statements, relevant for all people in every age, will now have to be understood as products of a certain culture and time. Phrases such as "of one substance with the Father" or "three persons and one God" have come from a Greek philosophy of the fourth century, unintelligible today to the people of Africa or Asia, not to mention our own young people. So our creeds may have to be changed in the light of new cultural contacts. Indeed, it is impossible to see how radically new insights about cultures will change our approach to belief. Are Christianity and the gospel one and the same thing? Or is Christianity a cultural product of the West, as Buddhism or Confucianism are of the East? Has not God been revealed in these faiths as well?

Conversion for those who live in a Western society can mean a growth in "holy and creative nonconformity" (Romans 12:2); an increasing expansion of our understanding of God's demand (to love God, and our neighbour as ourselves), as contrasted with the demands of the culture in which we live (consumerism, aggressive competition, anti-social individualism, exploitation of class, race, or sex, etc.).

No wonder, then, that Christians face a crisis in their faith and activity concerning mission. We are being compelled to rethink almost everything we have learned—a painful task indeed. Love of, and loyalty to, our leader Jesus Christ remain the same, but the paths along which Christ is leading us have become challenging new ones.

Yet we do not need to see this period of change in entirely negative terms. Crises can be positive experiences as well. The word *crisis* comes from a Greek verb which means 'to judge'. As David Paton wrote thirty-five years ago in a little book about the Christian experience of the Chinese revolution, God has judged the missionary movement and found it wanting. But the Greek word can also mean 'to choose' or 'to discern' (the English word *discriminate* comes directly from that Greek word). In Japan and other East Asian countries the word for crisis is written with two Chinese characters, one which means 'danger' (negative) and the other 'opportunity' (positive). Theologians in the Third World see this opportunity to choose as a unique and demanding *kairos*, a Greek word which denotes a moment in time when God calls the people to decide between two ways, one of life and one of death. So then, a crisis can be a chance for a new start, an opportunity to discern where God is leading us.

"Crisis in Mission" *Interpreting the Present Time: History, the Bible, and the Church's Mission Today,* Cyril H. Powles, © 1994 Anglican Book Centre, 600 Jarvis St., Toronto M4Y 2J6. Used with permission.

Appendix C

Centres offering Immunization Services

Each province now has a number of locations offering travel health services including immunizations. For a comprehensive list, please go to the Public Health Agency of Canada/Agence de santé publique du Canada: www.phac-aspc.gc.ca and click on Travel Health. In the United States, contact your regional Department of Health.

First-Aid Medical Kit

Here are some suggestions for things to pack in your first-aid kit. If you know that you will be traveling to an area where medical care is not readily available, you will want to pack emergency first aid supplies as well as the basics In addition, your family doctor may have some suggestions about additional contents based on your personal medical history.

Pack your medications and first-aid supplies in a water-proof and, ideally, insulated bag. Arrange in advance to have essential medical supplies with you in your carry-on luggage. New security regulations may limit the quantity or quality of liquids that you can carry on.

Basic Kit

Travel experts recommend taking the following items along on any trip:

thermometer
personal medications, both prescription and over-the-counter
aspirin, acetaminophen (for example, Tylenol), or ibuprofen (for example, Advil, Motrin)
sun block for skin and lips (SPF 15 or higher providing both UVA and UVB protection)
white iodine drops (for water purification, treatment of wounds)
condoms, birth control
bandages, butterfly closures
tensor bandage, triangular bandage/sling
extra eyeglasses or contacts, eyeglass repair kit, sunglasses
hearing aid batteries
small supply of toilet paper
moistened towelettes or small liquid hand sanitizer
sanitary supplies for menstruation
absorbent cotton
absorbent gauze
adhesive tape
alcohol swabs
antiseptic

burn ointment
disinfectant (zephiran, hydrogen peroxide)
insect sting emergency kit (*Ana-Kit or *Epipen) for known allergy
safety pins, scissors, tweezers, Swiss Army knife

Customized Kit

Travelers who will be living, working, or visiting remote areas, especially for long periods of time or in developing countries, should consider a kit that includes items from the list below that are appropriate to the climate, environment, or activities.

first aid manual
skin medications to relieve itching and sunburn
foot powder, moleskin
gauze (plain and elastic), non-adhering dressing
adhesive tape
latex gloves
disinfectant gauze
antibiotics, antihistamines, decongestant
vitamins (with fluoride)
laxative, antacid
motion sickness medication, altitude sickness medicine
oral rehydration salts
ear drops
eye antibiotic drops
topical corticosteroids and anti-fungals
adrenaline auto-injector
suture kit
venom extractor pump
disposable syringes and needles (ten of 3ml and five of 5ml with #22 or 23 needles), with the physician's accompanying letter*
insect repellant (with at least 30% DEET—don't apply a product that is more than 35% DEET to the skin, apply instead to clothing)
petroleum jelly
pecac syrup to induce vomiting in the event of oral poisoning
*Check with your doctor. It may be best to decline needle injections and opt for oral treatment whenever possible.

Dental Kit

Get a dental checkup and cleaning before leaving on your trip. Simple dental first aid supplies such as these are available in drugstores:
dental mirror
topical medication for mouth sores or sore gums
oil of clove (applied on the tooth) for tooth pain
cotton swabs and gauze.

Medications	Examples
Antacid	Diovol
Antibiotic	*Bactrim, *Septra (These are not to be used during pregnancy, for young children or if allergic to sulfa) *Cipro *Vibramycin
Antihistamines	Benadryl
Antimalarials	Depends on whether you are in a low-risk or high-risk area; consult your travel clinic.
Cough medicine	Robitussin DM
Decongestant	Nasal: Otrivin, General: Coricidin D
Diarrhea	Imodium Gastrolyte, Pedialyte or home-made rehydration solution: Add to 1 litre of purified water: 2 Tbsp. (1 hand scoop) of sugar 1/4 tsp. (1 three-finger pinch) of salt 1/4 tsp. of bicarbonate of soda (or another 1/4 tsp of salt if bicarbonate not available 1/2 cup of orange juice or a squeeze of lemon (for potassium replacement and taste.)
Earache	Auralgan
Eye/Ear infection	Polysporin eye/ear drops
Eye infection	Sodium Sulamyd
Fever/Pain	Tylenol, Aspirin
Laxative	Senokot
Skin care	Antibiotic: Bactroban Antiseptic: Phisoderm, Betadine, Dettol, Hibitane Itching: Caladryl lotion, Calamine Antifungal cream/powder: Canesten, Mycil, Micatin
Throat lozenges	Benylin Lozenges
Toothache	Anbesol, oil of cloves (on cotton acts as a local anaesthetic until on can get to a dentist)

*A doctor's prescription is needed to obtain these drugs.

Keep the following note in your first-aid kit in case you are scrutinized!questioned at border crossings.

To Whom It May Concern   Date

[Traveller's name] is carrying in his/her personal possession a medical kit, prescription medications and disposable needles and syringes to be used by a physician for safe administration of medication, if required, while overseas. These items are for this person's individual use and are not for re-sale.

Sincerely,
Physician's Name, Address

Adapted from *Health Advice for Overseas Travel*, Health Support Service, © CUSO, 1999.

Appendix D
Culture Shock

The expression "culture shock" may not deserve to be weeded out and purged from the literature of the field of culture learning, but its overuse has led to unfortunate negative connotations. Surely there is such a thing as intercultural conflict. Surely there is such a condition as inadequate competency. Surely there is such a state as intercultural incomprehension. Any combination of these can result from improper or inadequate preparation. But to call this syndrome "culture shock" diverts attention from more important matters. It can lead ultimately to educational approaches that are less a matter of preparation than of remediation—patching up and gluing back together rather than adequately preparing in the first place.

What would happen if the idea of "marriage shock" became popular? Surely there are profound adjustments to be made when two persons bring their separate identities and contrasting life histories and value systems into a commitment to unity. Or parenthood—is there anything in life that so predictably turns out to be much more demanding than was anticipated? But do we talk about "parenthood shock?" The term "culture shock" has been with us for over a quarter of a century, and it is not likely to go away Those who teach and write in this field do talk about it, whether or not we believe that it is a good idea to do so. It is a popular way to look at the matter, so we play along.

Fear is a strong motivator. Fear of the unknown is especially easy to exploit. Even among people who ought to know better, there is a tendency to play on the anxieties of people who need help. What is needed far more than the rude act of shaking sleepers into startled fear is helping them cope with what they will find when they awaken!

Three Shock Absorbers

What can be done to make culture shock less severe? In workshops for people going overseas, we try to develop three skills—empathy, observation and exploration.

Empathy

How a person relates to others is the foundation of cross-cultural effectiveness. Can you trust others? Do you accept help from others? Do you try to feel life from the point of view of the other person? Many North Americans place great importance on being independent and having their own way. That may work out fairly well in our own country, but there are very few places outside North America and Europe where independence is socially accepted. In most of the world, especially the third world nations, people are expected to need each other, especially within the extended family to which they happen to belong. This sort of mutually-dependent relationship is built on sensitivity to the needs and feelings of others.

One of the more useful ways to assess your level of empathy is to isolate some behavior or attitude you see in someone else and try hard to think of a possible reason why the other person does this or feels this way. You'll know that empathy is emerging when you begin to be really generous and nonjudgmental. You'll begin to make up alibis and excuses in your mind for other people, and you'll be more willing to see their side of the story

Observation

Observation games and drills can dramatically increase perceptual skills in a number of ways, often within a short period of time. Test yourself with the following exercise: close your eyes and reconstruct the setting in which you are now located. With your eyes still closed, try to spot something in your recall of the general scene that you haven't already thought about. Why is that window down from the top? How did that paint get scraped? Who might have left that small green object over there in the corner? Why? And so on. Then take a very quick peek out the window or off to the left and start the game again.

If you repeat this exercise several times a day over a period of weeks, you will find that your skill is increasing. As a bonus, you will develop a lot more self-confidence about your ability to observe. You will enjoy awareness of the interesting little questions that can be raised about things otherwise taken for granted. Perhaps the greatest value lies in learning the usefulness of asking yourself, "Why?" Even as a child asks "Why?" because he or she wants to learn, you will find yourself carrying on a continuous internal inquiry about your own environment.

Transactional Exploration

Are you learning to deal with new and unknown experiences by relating to them experimentally? Rather than becoming rigid and frightened because you lack information, or becoming "lost" for lack of a model to copy, do you get actively involved and try out your hunches?

This "trying out" is what we call transaction: do something and see what happens. As a child you learned more this way than any other. You never lose this capability, though as you grow older you tend to depend more on previous experience and the knowledge it has built within you. When you encounter something really new, something that your past experience doesn't cover, you can always resort to transactional exploration. Make an effort to rediscover this tactic.

Scientifically, transactional exploration is called "inquiry learning" or "discovery learning." In common-sense terms, it involves finding out through trial and error. Though in cross-cultural matters you don't want to do too many things that are going to make matters worse, it is usually better to do than not to do—to act rather than to freeze up. When you freeze you stop learning!

Robert Kohls, an expert in the field of intercultural training and the Director of Training and Development for the International Communication Agency, draws a useful distinction between frustration ("uncomfortable, but short-lived") and "culture shock."

Frustration arises from the following:
- Ambiguity of a situation in which you find yourself
- Mismatch between your expectations and the reality of a situation
- Unrealistic goals which you now realize are out of reach
- Inability to see results
    - because need is simply too great
    - because the work to be done is beyond your skills and understandings
    - because the work to be done is in reality different from the view held by those who are defining your mission
    - because the amount of time available to you is inadequate (or your period of service too short) to see the slow-paced efforts
- Growing awareness that the wrong methods are being used to achieve the intended objectives

Culture shock, by comparison, is a longer and larger problem with the following characteristics:

- Culture shock does not result from a specific event or series of events. It comes instead from encountering ways of doing, organizing, perceiving, or valuing things which are different from yours and which threaten your basic, unconscious belief that your enculturated customs, assumptions, values, and behaviors are "right." It comes from being cut off from the cultural cues and known patterns with which you are familiar—especially the subtle, indirect ways you normally express feelings.
- Culture shock does not strike suddenly or have a single principal cause. Instead it is a cumulative, building up slowly from a series of small events that are difficult to identify It comes from these realities:

- living and /or working over an extended period of time in a situation that is ambiguous
- having your own values (which you had heretofore considered as absolutes) brought into question—which yanks your moral rug out from under you
- being continually put into position in which you are expected to function with maximum skill and speed but where the rules have not been adequately explained.

Kohls offers five ways of coping with culture shock:

1. Gather information: Keep looking for things you overlooked before. There is always more to see and to learn. Some of it will make sense.
2. Look for logical reasons behind the strange and the unfamiliar: What is most important is the consciousness that things aren't inherently irrational simply because you haven't yet made sense of them. Keep trying—with a positive and open outlook.
3. Fight off the temptation to take out your frustration on the people of the host country: Also avoid expatriates who talk and think this way. They will drag you down deeper into culture shock.
4. Discover and affiliate with a person of the host country who can help you interpret experience: Just as surely as language differences can be bridged by a good translator, a culture translator or "bridge person" can help you understand the mysteries. Don't depend exclusively on fellow Americans to provide this sort of help. Many misunderstandings can be passed from one North American to another. Learn to trust people of the host country.
5. Have faith in yourself and in the underlying good will of those in the host country: The most trying experience can turn out to be a valuable milestone if you don't give up—on yourself, or on others.

Appendix E

In case of emergency

Often in countries where embalming is not common, disposal of a body must occur within 24-hours of death. This does not leave much time to make decisions when you are in shock and under the incredible stress of grief. You and your spouse and/or family should talk about your wishes in the event of death. Cremation is an option if you would like some final connection with Canada. The return of ashes also allows family and friends to bring closure to an infinitely sad event.

General procedure for crisis situations

1. Follow the procedures as outlined on p. 61 for victims of violence.

2. Keep a chronology of events before, during and after the crisis:
   - write down everything you remember and everyone else remembers happening in as much detail as possible;
   - include who notified who, time, etc.

3. Keep a log of phone calls/meetings with:
   - local authorities
   - embassy
   - church or employment authorities

4. Be in touch with local church authorities. Keep a record of their intervention.

5. Keep in touch with other overseas personnel, local people, where the person worked, where she/he was last seen or taken.

6. Gather any information local people may have of the event. Avoid any contact that may endanger local people.

7. If a witness can make a statement, take it; get it in writing. If the person cannot sign or needs to remain anonymous for safety, write it yourself, describe the informant as, e.g., "a 50-year old farmer," then sign it as receiving the testimony of this witness, date it, indicate your location. Have the statement witnessed by one or two other expatriates (for the safety of local people). These witnesses should *hear* the statement made by the witness if at all possible.

When the crisis involves a death due to violence

1. If the body is to be returned to the country of origin—plan for an autopsy before making funeral arrangements; get necessary permissions, etc.

2. If the body is to remain in the country where death occurred—if an autopsy is not possible, get one or two doctors to examine the body. If they are afraid to be named, have an expatriate with medical knowledge witness the examination, sign, date and note place. If doctors are unwilling to do even this, get some expatriate with medical knowledge to examine the body and report on the following:
   - specify cause of death
   - specify nature of wounds (how many, where, how wounds entered and exited body, calibre of bullets)
   - specify how many wounds
   - look for signs of additional bruising, beating, torture, stab wounds, etc.
   - make a drawing to indicate wounds/injuries or
   - take pictures, if possibly, preferably in color

3. If possible, look for evidence at the site of death (bullet casings, etc.)

4. Have an expatriate hand carry a copy of the preliminary medical

exam or autopsy out of the country, with the photos, to your church or work organization

5. Hand carry clothing to North America in plastic bags for forensic report

6. Send a copy of autopsy/report and photos to your embassy in the country where the death occurred

Appendix F

Physical or sexual violence

In the case of physical assault of any kind, immediate medical attention should be sought first followed by legal support within the country if this is available. In the case of rape or physical violence, it is important to speak out about it. Anger expressed will enable you to come to terms with the violation, and reporting the incident is a crucial step in stopping the abuse either for yourself or the next victim.

When the victim is reluctant to seek help or tell the truth about the assault, it can perpetuate the assault and leave the individual victimized for a longer term. You must assess your needs and what you must do to overcome an assault overseas. What would you do in Canada to overcome an assault? Who would you confide in? Will discretion work in your favour or hinder your handling of the situation? Is adequate counseling available in your host country? It is paramount to work out a strategy with someone you trust that will be effective.

When back in Canada, ask your denomination to arrange professional counseling for you. Readjustment to Canada can be difficult enough without sorting through and dealing with harassment and assault problems. Don't feel guilty and don't be silent.

Women's reluctance to confront the issue stems from a number of valid fears. They are embarrassed or humiliated that they are the targets of sexually coercive behaviour and may in some way feel responsible. Women are intimidated as subordinates in a hierarchical system, fearing that direct confrontation would result in threats to their person. Women often don't want husbands, boyfriends, parents or children to know of the assault.

Physical harassment or assault in any form is an act of violence, anger, power. Often, a rejection of a male's advances is equated by that male as a failure of his manhood. The wounded male ego might react by escalating harassment to the stage of sexual coercion.

Most men never engage in sexual harassment. Their religious beliefs, ethical standards, moral values and personal code preclude extramarital sex or aggressive, unsolicited sexuality. Certainly, it is unfair and unnecessary to judge all men based on the violations of a few. Those men who do perpetrate harassment or assault are committing a serious offense that needs to be addressed seriously.

10 Bibliography

There is no shortage of books and resources to help you in your preparation. Those listed here have been used by the Forum and by its member denominations. Though some have been around for many years, they continue to be used by mission personnel and so we include them here.

Please visit the Canadian Churches' Forum for Global Ministries at www. ccforum.ca for new resources as they are released.

Bridges, William *Transitions: Making Sense of Life's Changes.* Addison-Wesley. 2004. Helps to identify and cope with critical changes in our lives, offering skills, suggestions and advice for negotiating important passages.

CUSO. *Health Advice for Living Overseas.* CUSO. Ottawa, ON www.cuso.org. Practical and thorough guide with extensive lists of web and printed resources for caring for your health. Available from the Canadian Churches' Forum for Global Ministries. www.ccforum.ca

DuPont HL, Steffen R. *Textbook of Travel Medicine and Health*, 2 ed, BC Decker Inc. 2001. This comprehensive text provides guidelines and recommendations to help prevent disease and assure optimal medical treatment for travelers. Travel related topics covered include the environment and modes of travel, health promotion and disease prevention, travel for disadvantaged persons, malaria and other tropical and febrile illnesses, HIV/AIDS, sexually transmitted diseases, diarrhea, hepatitis, psychoneurologic disorders, and accidents.

Elmer, Duane. *Cross-Cultural Conflict: Building Relationship for Effective Ministry.* 1993. and *Cross-Cultural Servanthood: Serving the World in Christlike Humility.* 2006. Intervarsity Press. Both offer practical guidance for serving interculturally with sensitivity and humility.

Foyle, Marjory *Overcoming Missionary Stress.* Evangelical Missions Information Service, P.O. Box 794 Wheaton, Il. 60189 USA.
Beginning with a general understanding of stress experienced by overseas Christian workers, this book outlines the specific stress associated with living overseas as a single person, as a married couple or as a parent working overseas with children.

Freire, Paolo. *Pedagogy of the Oppressed.* Continuum International Publishing.

Kohls, L. Robert. *Survival Kit for Overseas Living.* 4th edition. 2001. Intercultural Press Inc. Offers basic strategies for getting to know hosts, managing culture shock, and developing intercultural communication skills as well as guidelines on how to deal with reverse culture shock when returning home.

Lingenfelter, Sherwood. *Ministering Cross-Culturally: An Incarnational Model for Personal Relationships.* 2nd edition. Baker Publishing. 2003. Examines the tension and conflict possible when missionaries attempt to work with people who come from different cultural and social backgrounds and uses model of basic values to assist individuals in managing those tensions.`

Longacre, Doris J. *Living More With Less.* Hearld Press, 1980, Kitchener, ON N2G 4M5
A practical guide for those trying to live simply, including subjects such as money, clothing, homekeeping, transportation, travel, celebrations and recreation.

Mission as Transformation: Welcoming the Stranger. Toronto: ABC Publishing, Anglican Book Centre. Collection of essays about God's mission in the world written by people who, in diverse ways, answered the call to participate in that mission.

Thomas, David. C and Kerr Inkson. *Cultural Intelligence: Living and Working Globally.* Berrett-Koehler Publishers. 2009. Illustrated with real-life stories, this book promises to help you become more effective in making decisions, communicating, and collaborating with others who are culturally different.

ONLINE
Government of Canada. Department of Foreign Affairs with links to Health Canada (www.voyage.gc.ca/dest/ctry/reportpage-en.asp)

US State Department with links to Center for Disease Control http://travel.state.gov/travel/cis_pa_tw/cis_pa_tw_1168.html

Intercultural Press, Inc. http://www.interculturalpress.com
Books and training materials that help professionals, businesspeople, travelers and scholars understand the meaning and diversity of culture. You will find country guides and culture guides as well books on the expatriate experience, global business, travel writing, as well as important tools for trainers and professional development.

International Bulletin of Missionary Research. http://www.internationalbulletin.org/ Great source for Christian history and analysis.

Missionary Care: Resources for Missions and Mental Health. Brochures, e-books, and other resources on all topics related to missons and well-being available to view online or to download.

Mission to Mission (www.missiontomission.org). From Mission to Mission assists those returning from cross-cultural mission to value that experience and to recognize their future life directions as a continuation of their Christian call to mission. Many resources available to both short and long-term mission personnel.

MK2MK (www.mk2mk.org) As a member care organization, MK2MK provides conferences around the world for MKs (mission kids) to come together and share their vast experiences, and to bond in their similarities of growing up overseas. MK2MK also seeks to care for MKs by providing a variety of resources to mission kids at many stages.

Anglican Church of Canada www.anglicancommunion.org and www.anglican.ca/about/departments/partnerships/index.htm

Evangelical Lutheran Church in Canada www.elcic.ca/In-Mission-In-the-World/

Evangelical Lutheran Church in America www.elca.org/Who-We-Are/Our-Three-Expressions/Churchwide-Organization/Global-Mission.aspx

Presbyterian Church in Canada www.presbyterian.ca/ministry/world

Presbyterian Church USA http://gamc.pcusa.org/ministries/world-mission/

Reformed Church in America www.rca.org/mission

Scarboro Foreign Missions www.scarboromissions.ca

United Church of Canada www.united-church.ca/partners/global

WEBSITES

Government of Canada. Department of Foreign Affairs with links to Health Canada (www.voyage.gc.ca/dest/ctry/reportpage-en.asp)

Intercultural Press, Inc. http://www.interculturalpress.com Books and training materials that help professionals, businesspeople, travelers and scholars understand the meaning and diversity of culture. You will find country guides and culture guides as well books on the expatriate experience, global business, travel writing, as well as important tools for trainers and professional development.

Link Care Missionary Services (www.linkcare.org) Link Care provides numerous services to missionaries and their organizations. These services range from the Restoration/Personal Growth program, to training and consultation services, to crisis debriefing services. Free resources including "How to Help Missionaries Return" and "The effects of burnout."

Mission to Mission (www.missiontomission.org). From Mission to Mission assists those returning from cross-cultural mission to value that experience and to recognize their future life directions as a continuation of their Christian call to mission. Many resources available to both short and long-term mission personnel.

MK2MK (www.mk2mk.org) As a member care organization, MK2MK provides conferences around the world for MKs (mission kids) to come together and share their vast experiences, and to bond in their similarities of growing up overseas. MK2MK also seeks to care for MKs by providing a variety of resources to mission kids at many stages.

Anglican Church of Canada (www.anglicancommunion.org) and (www.anglicancommunion.org/tour/index.cfm)

Evangelical Lutheran Church in Canada (www.elcic.ca/mission/index.html)

Presbyterian Church in Canada (www.presbyterian.ca/international/index.html)

Scarboro Foreign Missions (www.scarboromissions.ca)

United Church of Canada (www.united-church.ca/sharingpeople/overseas